Sales Secrets

Sales Secrets

✦

Proven Strategies for Increasing Sales

Mark Shaughnessy

iUniverse, Inc.
New York Lincoln Shanghai

Sales Secrets
Proven Strategies for Increasing Sales

iUniverse, Inc.

For information address:
iUniverse, Inc.
2021 Pine Lake Road, Suite 100
Lincoln, NE 68512
www.iuniverse.com

ISBN: 0-595-30192-4 (pbk)
ISBN: 0-595-66141-6 (cloth)

Printed in the United States of America

Contents

Acknowledgements

Thanks to all the great teachers and writers who provided me the knowledge, inspiration and guidance that allowed me to achieve more than I could have on my own.

For those authors where I used material that I had read over the years but cannot identify the specific writer, I thank you for allowing me to share your wisdom.

The people at iUniverse have been very helpful in getting this book ready to publish, most especially Rachel Weidel who guided me through the review process. Thanks to Jack Botts, the copyeditor who made insightful recommendations that improved the text and readability of *Sales Secrets*.

Thanks to all the sales reps who provided me the challenges that required me to study the field of sales and sales management.

I want to acknowledge those special sales reps who succeeded when others failed, who tried my ideas though sometimes doubted them, and to those who continued to use these techniques in their career.

A special thanks to Shannon Annis who provided me ideas on the concept and offered insight that encouraged me to continue this pursuit to completion.

Thanks to my children who left me alone in the evenings so I could spend the hours to finish this book. They would only interrupt me if they could find no other alternative for what they needed.

A special thanks to my wife Lisa who made suggestions and helped with designing the graphics so they were more useful to the reader.

Finally, thanks to you readers for purchasing the book and using these secrets to achieve success.

Introduction

Sales Secrets was developed with a few simple objectives for sales people: to increase sales, to provide a sales process that has been used successfully and to make the process simple to understand.

This book is designed to be a handy resource so sales people can readily refer to it and gain valuable ideas on a number of sales techniques.

Charts are provided to allow the reader to develop their personal sales and marketing plans. Some pages can be copied for continued use. In effect, this book becomes a workbook that can be used continually to assess progress, develop plans and manage work.

References are made to a number of books, audiotapes and other resources that should be read, listened to and pursued to provide a deeper understanding of each topic.

The book was written with the goal of providing as much information in fewer pages than most books so it can be read often in very little time.

It can be reviewed periodically when a salesperson experiences a slow sales period, or more importantly, when a salesperson is ready to make a quantum leap in sales results.

Each topic is comprehensive so a sales person can better understand, both for the first time and as a reminder, the ideas so important to sales success.

There is an old saying that the stronger the foundation, the higher the building. Thus, when establishing goals, you must have a solid foundation on which to build your objectives. The remainder of this book is designed to help you build a foundation for success.

As Henry Ford said, *"If you believe you can or believe you can't, in both cases you are probably right."*

When you believe you can achieve your goals, you will be successful in both your personal and professional life.

Sales Secrets is about preparing you for the challenges and opportunities that are in every market. Just as major leagues have preseason practice, we all must take time each year to revisit basic skill sets and get back to the fundamentals of prospecting, presenting and closing.

By using these techniques and making the commitment to be the best in the business, you can surpass your sales targets every year.

When companies apply these concepts, they will experience top-line revenue that will yield greater profits and continued growth within their organization.

When you apply these ideas, you will be assured of increased sales, a better quality of life and greater advancement in your career.

This book will provide the first step in that journey toward great success. If you plan to make it happen and make the commitment, the material provided will enable you to become more accomplished in the coming years and allow you to achieve even greater sales success throughout your career.

Take the challenge to be the best sales person you are capable of being by learning your craft. Commit to being the most professional sales person you can be, and you will be successful beyond your dreams.

1

Success Secrets

"Feed a person a fish and he can eat for a day.
Teach a person to fish and he eats for a lifetime."

If you were challenged to double your sales in this coming year over the prior one, could you do it? Before you say "no way," think about it for a moment. A number of techniques have enabled other sales people to be successful year after year.

An old Chinese proverb says, "You can't leap a chasm in two bounds." That is, if you truly want to be highly successful, you must make quantum leaps in your approach to sales, not just incremental changes in the way you do business. You don't want to grow by ten percent each year; but by fifty percent or more, even doubling sales each year.

A number of time-proven techniques can be applied to enable each person to become increasingly more successful, and these are explored in the following pages.

MAKE THE COMMITMENT

One of the most critical first steps in achieving your goals is to commit to them. Most people don't fully commit to an objective, rather they say they would like to have something, but don't take the necessary actions to make it happen.

First, in order to accomplish sales goals, you must commit to being one of the top sales people in your company and in your industry.

Like having ham and eggs for breakfast; the chicken is involved, but the pig is committed.

To accomplish your goals, you must believe you can achieve them. "You must believe it before you see it," to quote Dr. Wayne Dyer, a noted author of many self-development books.

DESIRE TO BE THE BEST

Typically, a sales person looks at the average performers and establishes sales targets based on average results.

Conversely, the sales leader sets targets based on the highest performer in terms of dollar sales, units or cases and seeks ways to exceed prior milestones.

The superstar will seek to achieve goals that have never been reached before, and will develop specific strategies for accomplishing them.

"The world stands aside to let anyone pass who knows where he is going." David Starr Jordan.

Of course, successful people always want to improve, and they can learn from their peer group. As a leading sales person in your company, you can still learn from other industry sales leaders by attending conferences and trade shows and by listening to other speakers.

By analyzing leader's strategies, one gains an understanding of how to achieve success and exceed expectations.

LAW OF ATTRACTION

The Law of Attraction declares that as you set your sights on an almost impossible goal, circumstances emerge that are totally unexpected that allow you to achieve your desired objective.

That is, no one person can spell out all the details of how the mission will be accomplished, but if you keep your eye on the goal, other factors and unforeseen opportunities will arise that enable you to achieve your unique vision.

KNOW YOUR SALES STYLE

Those who appear to be good sales persons or who have been told that they would be good in sales often discover they are in the wrong sales position. Primarily, there are sales people who are suited for inside sales and those who are more outside oriented.

Those better suited to an inside sales position are more comfortable when customers come to that person, like retail sales, where the store advertising creates the customer demand.

Those who need to be more active and reach out to their prospects are best suited as outside sales persons who create opportunities. They tend to socialize easily at parties and take the initiative when meeting others.

The outside sales person has no call reluctance and is willing to cold call on others via the telephone or in person. Call reluctance, the fear of calling strangers or clients, prevents a person from being successful in outside sales.

The willingness to call new prospects to get an appointment, to stop by a prospects office unannounced, or ability to sell over the phone is a strong attribute of an outside sales person or a telemarketer.

Either role can be successful, and when people are put into the appropriate position for which they are best suited, they will be able to reach their full potential. It is important to know the best sales role where you can succeed in order to achieve your greatest success in a sales position.

MIRRORING

One popular method of achieving the same success as other sales leaders is "mirroring," or doing what successful people do. Observe what they do and how they do it, and copy their activities to achieve greater success.

It is likely that there are sales people in your organization who sell more than you do; perhaps double the amount that you produce. How do they do it?

One of the first secrets of mirroring is to invite the top sales person to lunch and ask them what they do that is different from what you do. They often provide tips on what would improve your effectiveness.

Areas that may need improvement include: time management, returning phone calls in a timely way, preparing for presentations, and closing skills. A number of suggestions, if identified and corrected, could put you on the right track.

Perhaps you can join them for a day on sales calls to view their presentation techniques or listen to their telephone prospecting.

Sales leaders are not selfish and they are willing to help others. Top performers are like professional golfers who give other golfers tips that may result in the recipient doing better than the advice-giver. They both feel better for it.

MENTORING

Mentoring is another method in which a person engages with a more successful person and uses this experienced resource to provide observations, guidance and direction.

THE MASTERMIND PRINCIPLE

A popular and effective method is to be part of a "mastermind" group that meets regularly to share ideas, problems and solutions.

Brainstorming sessions allow ideas to surface, encouraging a number of solutions to emerge for further consideration. The secret to brainstorming is to allow ideas to flow freely and not to judge them as they are presented.

This step ensures each person is encouraged to submit ideas, no matter how silly or offbeat they may seem at that time. Only after all ideas have been submitted will they be discussed in any detail.

Meeting once a month for breakfast or lunch can prove invaluable in developing insight and creative ideas for improving your skills. Sales leaders and those who aspire to sales success can take the initiative by developing their own mastermind group to discuss sales ideas, marketing concepts and product knowledge.

This peer group can explore issues that one would not feel comfortable discussing with their sales manager. And this forum can raise product, pricing and customer service issues that can be channeled through management to better inform the company of the marketplace needs.

Napoleon Hill, who studied and wrote about the most successful men of the twentieth century, describes the mastermind concept in detail in his classic book, *Think and Grow Rich*.

SPEED TO MARKET

It is imperative that you get to your prospects first with your solutions. Those who have mastered this strategy have become more successful in achieving the desired sales results.

There are numerous examples in business of companies and individuals who delivered their product before others and dominated their market. Some examples are Thomas Edison with the light bulb and

Henry Ford with the automobile for the masses, but more recent examples includes Microsoft and Dell.

The title of a recent book says it all, and the contents are worth reading. *It's not the BIG that eat the SMALL, it's the FAST that eat the SLOW*, by Jason Jennings & Laurence Haughton.

You don't want to hear from prospects that they wished they had heard from you a couple months ago when they were making their buying decision.

Get your name out in the marketplace and keep it in front of your prospects through mass marketing, letter campaigns, advertising and other means that will be explored later.

PEAK TO PEAK SELLING

Peak to peak selling is used by the sales professional to maintain consistency in producing sales results. That is, make a sale regularly, whether it is daily, weekly, monthly or annually.

The secret to avoiding the valleys in the sales cycle is to make a sale on consistent basis. Peaks and valley selling is an emotional roller coaster to be avoided.

Be consistent in producing sales results.

QUESTIONING AND LISTENING

Developing the ability to ask questions and listen to others is a trait among successful people. They become more informed, better able to nurture relationships and achieve more than those who don't.

Asking questions allows you to understand a prospect's challenges and enables you to prepare a more targeted solution to satisfy a customer's needs.

An excellent book, *Socratic Selling* by Kevin Daley and Emmet Wolfe, explains these traits in more detail.

"Wisdom is the reward you get for a lifetime of listening when you'd preferred to talk."—Doug Larsen.

Listening is a lost art and is one of the most important traits of a successful sales person. Although the stereotype sales person is one who makes a "pitch," in reality, the person who listens for the underlying challenges will surpass others in achieving superior sales results.

CRITICAL SUCCESS FACTORS

These CSFs are vital for a person to achieve success and all of these play an important part in realizing your personal and professional goals.

Critical Success Factors
1. **Goal Setting.**
2. **Time Management.**
3. **Sales & marketing.**
4. **Prospecting.**
5. **Presenting.**
6. **Negotiating.**
7. **Communication.**

These are key topics that will be addressed in the following chapters, and it is vital that you become an expert in each area in order to achieve maximum results.

ALIGN OBJECTIVES WITH ORGANIZATION

Your objectives should align with the rest of the organization to ensure that resources are available to support your sales efforts.

If you plan that eighty percent of your sales will be product A, but you sell eighty percent of product B, you may find a shortage of supplies and inadequate staff to service your new customers.

And, the company profit objectives may be compromised if you don't sell the appropriate product mix. Often, each product has different profit margins, and the company develops its corporate profit objectives based on expected sales of each product line.

When you learn that you have a number of prospects that are different than the original sales plan, inform management so it can take the necessary steps to align resources to support your sales efforts.

By selling the right mix of products you ensure that the company will be able to fulfill the customers' expectations and meet your company's objectives.

COMMIT TO PERSONAL DEVELOPMENT

As part of your personal development plan, prepare a comprehensive training program that will ensure that you are fully trained in all aspects of the business. If your company does not support these needs, then you must seek them on your own.

In addition to product knowledge, focus on sales skills, presentation techniques, negotiating strategies, computer skills and communication abilities. You want to be the total rep, not just a great sales person.

"Knowledge is the food of the soul." Plato.

Studies show that those who consistently read, listen to tapes and develop their professional skills achieve far more than their counterparts who don't invest in personal improvement.

Read every day

Reading a book each month will have a powerful impact on a person's life in a short period of time. Most people do not read one book a year, and that leaves average people behind their peers.

Successful people read one hour every day. This can be easily accomplished by reading a chapter in the morning or at night prior to going to bed, and you will finish one book every two to four weeks.

By reading how others accomplished their goals or overcame obstacles, you will generate new ideas for approaching your work. Reading triggers thoughts that are not always directly related to the task at hand but provide solutions as your mind becomes attracted to new ideas.

"Those who don't read are no better off than those who can't."—Brian Tracy.

Books on sales and sales management help you understand what you should be doing and how it should be completed and what others expect from you. Books on leadership provide an overall perspective on business and ethics.

Provide yourself the foundation for more effectively communicating with others while giving yourself sound ideas on improving your personal performance.

Publications such as the Wall Street Journal, Forbes, Fortune and Business Week keep you abreast of the current events and also provide in depth articles on successful companies and individuals.

By continually reading, you remain updated on what is occurring in your company, the industry and the general economy. What's more, this greater understanding will enable you to speak more confidently about company and industry strategies. This unique advantage separates you from other sales reps and builds credibility when talking with prospects, customers and distributors.

"I cannot live without books." Thomas Jefferson.

A list of business books in *Business Week, USA Today* or the list provided in the reference section of this book includes must-read business classics.

Listen to audiotapes

Audiotapes are effective for gaining valuable information while in your car, exercising or in the office. You can obtain tapes through Nightingale-Conant at www.nightingaleconant.com, the world leader in self-development audio programs for forty-three years.

Personal training plan

The professional sales person seeks additional training throughout their career by attending sales seminars on strategic selling such as Miller-Heiman, time management sessions like Franklin Covey and presentations skills offered in their local community.

Personal Development Plan:

- Presentation training.
- Product knowledge.
- Phone skills.
- Communication skills.
- Technology.
- Time management.

List the books you plan to read and the audiotapes you will listen to this coming year. See adjoining page for a chart to track your progress.

Also list and commit to specific programs you will attend this coming year:

- Franklin Covey time management.
- Miller Heiman sales strategies.
- Sandler Sales Institute.
- Brian Tracy seminar.
- Telemasters telephone training.
- Microsoft Outlook training session.

PERSONAL DEVELOPMENT PLAN

Books	Audiotapes

TECHNOLOGY

Using technology tools, such as laptop computers, cell phones, Power-Point, video conference, e-mail, the Internet and your website will greatly improve your effectiveness. Although many companies provide these tools, they are often not used. Typically, less than twenty percent of the capabilities of each are used, which limits the efficiency and effectiveness of you and your organization.

Internet presentations

Making presentations via the Internet rather than in person is becoming more commonplace by using technology like Placeware, Mindarrow and Genysys.

Sales force automation

Tools are readily available to enhance your planning, prospecting and data collection. You can easily prepare mailing lists, sort prospects by territory and update your contact information quickly. Sales activity and expense reports can be prepared in minutes when the information is entered regularly.

Some prominent software includes:

- Goldmine.
- ACT!.
- Pivotal.
- Maximizer.
- Microsoft Outlook.
- Lotus Notes.

Look in magazines such as *Success* or *Sales and Marketing Management* for more information.

CELL PHONES

Cell phones are now a required accessory that allows you to respond more quickly and are a handy reference tool for phone numbers, background information on clients, your territory, sales results and other relevant data.

Secrets for cell phone usage include:

- Never take another call while you are with a client or prospect.
- Never take a different call when you are on the phone with your boss.
- Always answer the call when your spouse or children call.

INCREASE SELLING TIME

Less than thirty percent of an average salespersons time is spent selling. Your goal should be to spend more than fifty percent of your time selling if you are an outside sales person and more than eighty percent for inside sales reps.

Tom Hopkins, in his classic book, *How to Master the Art of Selling*, wrote, "Selling time is when a sales person is meeting with a prospect that has the authority to buy. Otherwise, it is just activity."

Eliminate time spent on casual conversations, interruptions, meetings and personal calls.

Work while at work and maximize your selling time to achieve your personal and professional sales goals.

SCHEDULE PLANNING TIME

Schedule time each day to plan such activities as prospecting, reviewing proposals, returning phone calls or preparing for a presentation.

Review your prospect lists, clients and distributors at the end of each day. Within one month you will develop a habit of reviewing your daily work for the next day resulting in being thoroughly prepared and enthusiastic about the possibilities.

Initially, plan on taking Friday afternoons off from selling and use that time to review your territory, complete expense and activity reports, update your customer and prospect lists and read industry literature to ensure that you remain current.

As you become more proficient, you will find that Friday afternoons are excellent times to contact those hard-to-get prospects, as they too are spending that time on planning activities.

DEVELOP SUCCESS HABITS

In order to develop successful habits, you must stick to the new ideas continually until they become second nature.

There is a simple theory that if you practice a new technique for twenty-one days, it will become an acquired habit. Examples include reading an hour a day, planning the next day at the end of the prior day, and prospecting each week.

By following and adhering to winning principles, you will develop the proper habits to ensure greater success.

GET OFF TO A GREAT START

A study concluded that sales people in their first year of business tend to do the same throughout their career.

That is, if they start fast, they are successful for years. Conversely, when sales people get off to a slow start in their first year, they remain behind for years.

Those that are most successful learn their products quickly, study the sales process and identify their key customers and prospects. Moreover, these reps talk with leading reps to learn the best practices, make joint calls with top sales people and sales managers and they sell something. That is, they get on the scoreboard and learn the implementation process.

In short, make the special effort to get a sale that provides the confidence and momentum to excel.

CODE OF ETHICS

Following a strong code of ethics in business means that you do not talk negatively about your competitors, that you sell only what your company is able to support and that you meet all commitments made to your customers. Anything less, and you will not achieve success and may wind up moving from company to company.

DO IT NOW!

Start using these techniques today, and you will begin to experience success immediately. Do not hesitate in taking the steps necessary to become successful. Commit to becoming a sales success now. Read this and other recommended books and take action to improve your sales techniques.

"Give the best that you have to the highest you know, and do it now." Ralph W. Sockman.

Don't get paralysis through analysis. Begin to incorporate these ideas and concepts into your daily work. Do It Now!

SUCCESS SECRETS

1. Make the commitment to sales success.

2. Follow the law of attraction.

3. Know your sales style.

4. Use mirroring/mentoring techniques.

5. Develop a mastermind group.

6. Speed to market is vital.

7. Develop peak-to-peak strategy.

8. Enhance questioning and listening skills.

9. Improve on your critical success factors.

10. Align objectives with organization.

11. Commit to personal development.

12. Develop technology skills.

13. Increase selling time.

14. Schedule planning time.

15. Adopt success habits.

16. Get off to a great start.

17. Follow high code of ethics.

18. Do it now!

2

Goal-Setting Secrets

Most people, and nearly all-sales people, are not effective at the goal-setting process. Typically, a sales manager assigns a sales quota, and sales reps try harder than the prior year and hope to achieve more in the coming year.

Hope Is Not A Strategy by Rick Page presents a thoughtful approach to selling complex, high tech products and services and was widely endorsed by all sales reps who read it. Rick Page is a personal trainer to more than 25,000 sales super stars.

Successful sales people take a different approach from just hoping for success. They clearly define their goals and develop specific strategies for accomplishing them. This is a goal achievement process rather than simply goal setting.

Each person faces unique challenges, but you can surpass your objectives by developing personal sales goals based on skill levels, market potential and sales strategies.

Most successful companies and successful sales people use the following process. Although some reps resent the thought process, it should be embraced and adopted for use throughout your career.

GOAL SETTING PROCESS

The first step is to determine what you want to achieve, whether it is in your professional career or your personal life.

Most sales people want to achieve their sales goals, whether it is in units, revenue or being the top performer in the company, but they often lack a game plan for achieving them.

Salespeople, left alone to set their own goals or quota, often set them much higher than management does, and much higher than they have ever achieved, or in some cases, could ever achieve.

This does not mean you should restrict yourself in any way from achieving far beyond what your management expects or what others have accomplished or even what you have accomplished in the past.

When you know what you are trying to achieve in each area, then you can better achieve the positive balance in your life. To quote Alfred E. Newman, "Most folks don't know what they want, but they are pretty sure they don't have it."

People fail in the goal setting process by not determining *how* to achieve their desired goals. That is, what specific sales activity or actions must be completed to achieve their objectives?

"*In the absence of clearly defined goals, we are forced to concentrate on activity and ultimately become enslaved by it.*" Chuck Coonradt

Some view challenging goals as simply unattainable and give up. If you feel that way, then you will likely not achieve them, as that would prove you to be wrong.

QUANTUM LEAP STRATEGY

Those who desire superior results use all the following techniques *except* they increase their goals by ten fold or more. That is, rather than a goal of one million dollars in sales, the superior sales person sets a goal of *ten million or one hundred million in sales*. The strategies may be similar but they will view the challenge differently.

As you follow the steps in the subsequent pages, ask yourself what you could do to take it up another notch to achieve superstar status.

SMART METHOD FOR SETTING GOALS

The first step toward achieving your goals, is to ensure they meet the SMART test; Specific, Measurable, Agreed to, Realistic and Time based.

S-Specific. Be very clear in describing what you want to achieve. For example, "I will achieve one million dollars in sales this year."

M-Measurable. The goals must be quantifiable. That is, I will sell fifty units each year.

A-Agreed to, or Achievable. Does everyone agree that these can be achieved and are committed to them?

R-Realistic. Can you or anyone achieve the goals, or are they so far-fetched that you "plan to fail"?

T-Time-based. Goals must have a time frame for achieving them, such as this year, this quarter, this month, this week, this day, this hour, or right now.

An example of using the SMART method would be: "My goal is to sell $1 million of new revenue and make $100,000 in commissions this year." This goal is specific, measurable, agreed to, realistic and time-based. How to achieve these goals will require more exploration.

The superstar rep may set a goal of ten million dollars that may appear to be unrealistic and not achievable, but it could meet the other criteria. With additional thought to be explored later, a larger sales goal may be attainable.

HOW TO ACHIEVE GOALS

An approach is to view goals from three perspectives:

1. Barriers to success.

2. Breaking down goals.

3. Develop action steps.

Barriers to Success.

Identify the barriers that prevent you from achieving your sales goals. First, list the barriers that prevent you from achieving your desired success. Be honest. Determining the barriers not only include assessing your own skills, but also the product portfolio, customer service and other issues that are hurdles you must overcome.

Any of these barriers can derail your success and prevent you from achieving your desired success. Talk with your sales manager or sales leader and seek help in getting the assistance. It will make you more successful and will ease your workload as you become more effective in each area.

Your company can be a barrier to your success. Your ability to communicate to management how the company must support you include:

- Competitor's features and benefits.
- Are you price competitive?
- Do your systems provide efficiency?
- Are your Marketing campaigns effective?

List the barriers to your success and develop action steps to overcome them. Some examples include:

- List of prospects; do you know whom to call?
- Telephone skills; are you comfortable calling others?
- Communication skills; are you effective at letter writing, internal memos or email, etc.?
- Presentation skills; can you represent all your products and respond to questions?
- Do you fear closing the sale?
- Are you skilled at time/territory management?

BARRIERS	ACTION STEPS

Breaking Down Goals.

Most sales reps miss their goals either because they go for the big sale or they make a lot of smaller sales that don't add up to their quota.

In order to achieve your goals every year, you must have a consistent plan and not rely on one big sale to bail you out. You want to make your goals by selling consistently each month, and the big sale every year or two is just icing on the cake. Elephant hunting is the curse of the big game hunter: feast or famine.

"Nothing is particularly hard if you divide it into smaller jobs."—Henry Ford.

By breaking down goals from an annual goal to monthly goals and then weekly goals, the goals are more manageable.

That is, when you make them more bite-size, they are less intimidating, and you can develop a more realistic method for achieving them. For example, a $1 million-dollar goal can be broken down as follows:

Goals	Annual	Quarterly	Monthly	Weekly
$Dollar	$1.m	$250k	$84k	$21k
Unit sales	48	12	4	1

Action Steps to Achieve Goals.

Identify the key measurements that you must achieve monthly and weekly to reach your annual sales goals. These include increasing prospecting, improving your close ratio, and expanding your sales activity, among others.

Increase prospecting

If you know that you can make one sale each week by meeting with ten prospects, then you know that you have to plan your prospecting activities to achieve ten meetings a week.

Now you must develop steps so you will meet ten prospects per week. These may include:

- Mail out fifty letters per week.

- Telephone twenty prospects per week.

- Obtain ten quality referrals per week.

Improve your close ratio

The close ratio is the percent of time that you make a sale compared to the number of times you present your product or service.

If your close ratio is ten percent, and the leading sales person in your office has a close ratio of thirty percent, you know that you can triple your sales by improving your close ratio.

This can be accomplished using the techniques presented in this book and other reference materials. These would include improving your telephone techniques, presentation strategies, communication skills, time management and qualifying prospects.

You may also need to increase the number of letters sent, telephone calls, appointments, proposals and presentations.

In short, the ways to improve your close ratio is not just to be a better closer, it includes a number of factors working in harmony to be a sales superstar.

WRITE DOWN YOUR GOALS

Write down goals and keep them prominently displayed and you will be more driven to accomplish them. The more specific they are the better, so you can clearly visualize them. Some hang pictures of a favorite vacation location, of a car they wish to purchase or a home they would like to own.

Simply thinking that you want to be the sales leader and wanting to make a lot of money is not good enough. Sales leaders set clearly defined goals of being the top producer in the company and they state specifically how much money they expect to earn.

Case Study

A study at Harvard several years ago showed that of a graduating class, sixty-eight percent of the students didn't have defined goals, twenty-nine percent had stated their goals, but only three percent wrote out their goals. Thirty years later, the three percent who wrote down their goals accomplished more financially than all of the other students combined. The only difference was their willingness to write down their goals.

A sales rep took this exercise literally and wrote down his activity goals on three-by-five index cards, i.e., to contact twenty prospects each week.

Each Friday he listed his prospects, and during the following week he didn't stop until he contacted every one of them. While others were discussing where to go to lunch at 11:45, he was making one more call.

He listed his goals on his desk, on his mirror at home, in his coat pocket and on the back of his business card as a reminder. Guess who the leading sales rep was that year and for years to come?

TRACK SALES RESULTS

A simple but effective goal-setting process will yield your desired result. In our example, the sales rep wants to make $150,000 a year. If his salary is $50,000, the rest comes from commissions. Assuming the company pays ten percent commission on each sale, a $1,000,000 in sales yields $100,000 in commissions, or a total of $150,000.

Next, determine the number of units you must sell to achieve a million dollars in sales. If you sell four units a month, or forty-eight per year, then your average sale must be $21,000, or more than $84,000 per month.

Income Goals	
Income	$150,000
Salary	$50,000
Commission	$100,000
Sales	$1.0 million
# Units/Year	48
Avg. Sale	$21,000
Avg. Rev/Mo.	$84,000

If your average sale is less than $21,000, then you must either sell more units or increase your average sale. By knowing your numbers, you can better track your progress. Since most companies pay compensation on revenue, not units, you must focus on your revenue goals and results.

Track the number of units sold, total revenue per sale, and average revenue per sale. See adjoining chart.

Track Units, Revenue/Sale and Avg Revenue/Sale

Month	#Units	Revenue/Sale	Avg. Revenue/Sale
January			
February			
March			
April			
May			
June			
July			
August			
September			
October			
November			
December			

MONITOR SALES ACTIVITY

Once you have determined your sales goals by year, quarter, month and week, determine the level of sales activity required to generate the new sales.

A method to track your sales activity is to use the point system described in the must-read book, *How To Become a Rainmaker*, by Jeffrey J. Fox, a marketing consultant and author of other books, *How to Become a CEO* and *How to Become a Marketing Superstar*. He awards points for getting a lead or referral, gaining an appointment, meeting with a decision maker and closing a sale.

By improving your ratios, you will make quantum leaps in your ability to achieve greater success. When you track the results of your sales campaigns, monitor the number of proposals and presentations you deliver and improve your close ratio, you will experience more success while working less.

Remember that you cannot always control your sales results, but you can control your sales activity.

The critical sales activity measures are:

- *Close Ratio*
- *#Presentations*
- *#Proposals*
- *#Face Calls*
- *#Telephone Calls*
- *#Mailers*

Close ratio

The first step in determining your required level of activity is to calculate your close ratio. That is, how many sales do you make for every presentation, proposal or call you make. You may determine your close ratio in a number of ways as long as you are consistent.

If your close ratio is twenty percent, then you sell two accounts for every ten presentations you make. When you improve your close ratio, you increase your sales with the same level of sales activity.

Number of presentations

Presentations may be defined as making a formal presentation to a prospect, client or distributor for a specific account. This is different from a capabilities presentation that is provided as a general overview of your services. Tracking the number of presentations is particularly effective with a direct or captive sales force.

Track the number of presentations each week, month and quarter to determine how many you are making and how many result in sales.

Also, record the amount of time it takes to prepare for a presentation and the time to make it. A simple rule of thumb is to assume two hours per presentation and an equal amount of time for preparation. These times will vary based on the complexity of the sales call, travel time and the number of products offered.

Presentations can be the most time-consuming sales activity, but it can yield the greatest results. Secrets for making effective presentations will be explored in a later chapter.

Proposal activity

Proposals are written quotes that describe your product or service that may turn into a presentation. In some sales organizations, especially telemarketing or when using distributors, proposal activity is more important than face-to-face presentations.

Determine the number of proposals you need to send out to make the desired number of presentations each month. If you make a presentation on fifty percent of all proposals, you must send out forty proposals a month.

- 40 proposals per month.
- 50%-percent proposals result in presentations.
- 20 presentations per month.

To generate more sales, increase proposal activity and improve your presentation ratio.

Face calls

If you are an outside sales person, making face-to-face calls with prospects is an excellent way to build relationships, demonstrate your product and establish credibility.

In some businesses, finding people willing to meet with you is becoming increasingly difficult due to time constraints. Face-to-face meetings are expensive for your company to support, particularly when it requires travel.

Rather, qualifying leads, that is determining the best prospects that have an interest in your product or can afford it, is more important than before.

Qualifying leads through mailings, telephone, Internet, teleconferencing and video conferencing are more popular and cost-effective methods.

By using these techniques, you and the prospect can better assess if there is interest and if a proposal should be sent outlining the benefits and prices for your services.

Tracking face call activity allows you to determine how effective different marketing initiatives are and the impact on sales.

Telephone calls

If you use the telephone to generate leads or sales, assess your phone call activity. For example, how many phone calls does it take to get a face call meeting, or to send a proposal or to close a sale?

If it takes two phone calls to generate a proposal, then you must make about eighty calls a month to yield forty proposals each month. That may seem daunting, but with an average of twenty-two working days in a month, that is about four phone calls a day. If your phone calling ratios do not meet these standards, then you must improve your phone power skills.

- # Phone calls per proposal.
- # Calls per month.
- # Calls per day.

When you add up and review all the sales activity numbers, you will know how many phone calls it will take to meet your professional sales goals each year.

Mail Campaigns

A mail campaign is another method to generate leads. To determine the effectiveness of direct letter mailing campaigns, carefully track mailings and the number of resulting sales.

The secret is to use different letters or special offers and record the results of these varying sales campaigns. You should "test" to determine which initiative yields the greatest return. You may then decide to expand or reduce a campaign depending on the results.

We know that most returns on mailings are small, typically less than two percent, and increasing the return by one percent can have a significant impact on the results. A return of three percent is a fifty percent increase above average, or a very successful campaign.

Knowing the return rate will help determine how many mailers must be sent monthly to yield the desired results. Developing successful mailers and not just sending any letter is worth investing time and effort.

By tracking sales activity and results you can best assess where to spend your resources in your sales campaigns.

PERSONAL SALES PLAN

Sales representatives should develop a personal sales plan to include sales goals, sales strategies and activity measures. Focusing efforts on those defined objectives will maintain the required attention to ensure sales success.

Developing a sales plan will reveal a number of different methods to market products that were previously unforeseen. The process of developing and reviewing your plan create thoughts that otherwise would have been missed.

Goals, sales strategies and activity measures are critical to your personal sales plan. By defining each, you develop a plan that can be measured on a weekly, monthly, quarterly and annual basis.

All these are vital to have in one document so you can assess your progress and determine if you are taking the appropriate action steps that will lead to achieving your personal and professional goals.

Sales rep goal setting exercise

One sales rep was challenged when asked what his sales goals were. He said that he wanted to sell a lot of accounts. When asked why he wanted to sell a lot of accounts, he said he wanted to make a lot of money. When further challenged as to whether he wanted to sell a lot of accounts or make a lot of money, he said he wanted to make a lot of money.

Once the rep understood his true goals, he changed his strategy to focus only on larger accounts. Within one year, he was the leading sales rep in his division, and in the following three years he became the leading sales person in the entire company. He never lost his focus on what he wanted and how he was going to achieve his goals.

IN SUMMARY

Goal setting is the most critical step in achieving your personal and professional objectives. You must know what you want to achieve or you will simply be working aimlessly toward an unknown target.

Although using the SMART method for establishing goals is a good first step, challenge yourself by setting extremely high goals and develop strategies to achieve them. For example, you may want to sell a certain number of units and average a specific dollar amount each month, but also work on a major account or a joint venture that could yield significant revenue.

Allow yourself to dream about surpassing your own expectations and you will find ways to achieve these impossible goals. Allow the Law of Attraction to work for you.

Break down your goals into attainable amounts, write down your goals and strategies and monitor your sales activity to ensure you are doing the right things in order for you to achieve your desired objectives.

PERSONAL SALES PLAN

Sales Goals	Annual	Quarterly	Monthly
$Dollar			
#Units			
Avg Rev/Sale			

Activity Goals

- Mail twenty letters per week.
- Make twenty phone calls per week.
- Make five presentations per week.
- Make ten face calls per week.
- Generate ten proposals per week.
- Close one sale each week.

SALES GOALS

Personal Goal	Example	Your Goals
Compensation Goal	$150,000	
Salary	$50,000	
Commissions Goal	$100,000	
Sales Goal	$1 million	
Commission @10%	$100,000	
Monthly Sales Goal	$84,000	
#Sales per mo	4 sales	
$ Per Sale	$21,000	
Close Ratio	20%	
# Presentations	20/mo	
# Proposals	40/mo	
# Face Calls	40/mo	
#Telephone Calls	80/mo	
#Mailers	80/mo	

GOAL SETTING SECRETS

1. Goal setting is a process.

2. Develop a quantum leap strategy.

3. Goals must meet the SMART test.

4. Learn how to achieve goals.

    a. Break down goals.

    b. Identify barriers to success.

    c. Set action steps.

5. Write down your goals.

6. Track sales results.

    a. # Sales.

    b. Avg. revenue per sale.

    c. Avg. revenue per month.

7. Monitor sales activity.

    a. Track close ratios.

    b. # Presentations.

    c. # Monthly proposals.

    d. # Face calls.

    e. # Phone calls.

8. Develop personal sales plan.

3

Time Management Secrets

"It's more important to do the right things than to do things right."

—*Peter Drucker.*

According to virtually all time management books, you can gain one to two hours a day by using time management techniques. It is true.

It is also sadly true that people don't take the time to read books on time management or to plan their day. We all have the same amount of time, 1,440 minutes each day, but it is important how we use it. You may decide to spend more time selling, more time with your family, golfing or reading.

Improve the time you spend at home as well as at work. By using proven time management techniques, the return on time becomes greater. Moreover, you gain a sense of control over your professional and personal life while improving your effectiveness.

"Getting ready is the secret of success."—Henry Ford.

You can have peace of mind knowing that you can step back when pressured and create lists, prioritize them and complete the most important tasks.

Making lists and planning your time will result in being more effective and efficient.

Being more effective is doing the right things, that is, concentrating time and effort on those activities that give the greatest reward.

Being more efficient is doing things right. Examples include having a neat desk, having a color-coded filing system and ensuring all your reports are completed on time.

High achievers are more effective than efficient. They know that it is more important to focus their time on selling rather than less important tasks such as ensuring that their files are in order.

Successful sales reps know they must pick up the phone and talk to someone about their products, rather than making sure they have identified every prospect in their territory. Take action on those initiatives that will generate a sale, revenue and commission.

MASTER LIST

You will accomplish more when you have a system to track your activities. Developing a master list that includes everything you must complete enables you to review one central list to ensure that items are visible. This list is intended as a catch-all for all tasks to be completed.

Don't put them in order to start, just write them down and prioritize them later. By not prioritizing them when you are listing, you open up your mind to new ideas without judging them, which allows for greater output of ideas.

Once you have listed all items, you can refer to this list when deciding on what to complete. Other more focused methods are used for tracking completion of items.

GETTING ORGANIZED

To get organized, use organizers, note pads, journals or a daily list of To Dos. Other methods are: making folders for each month of the year and each day of the month and then putting the list of items on a note card and filing them in the corresponding date that an item should be worked on.

Using January through December folders, 1-31 manila files and To Do lists will track most tasks.

Some organizer companies that provide a full array of options include:

- Franklin Covey
- Day Timers
- Planner Pads

Using a popular hand-held personal digital assistant (PDA) can be effective, and items can be captured and prioritized for your effectiveness. PDA examples are: Palm Pilot and Blackberry.

Other organization tools are Microsoft Outlook and Lotus Notes. Both are effective for tracking projects, clients, email and a host of other functions.

PRIORITIZE WORK

Deciding on the order of completing the task is the easiest part but often the most overlooked aspect of effective time management. Assess the importance of each task and review the list daily to ensure that you remain focused on completing the most important and urgent tasks.

A-priority: Important and urgent.
B-priority: Important but not urgent.
C-priority: Urgent but not important.
D-priority: Not urgent and not important.

Prioritize your list by the most important task as being an A-1, then A-2, and so forth. Work on the A-1 task until you complete it or cannot work any further on it, and then go to A-2, etc.

Some examples of A priorities include:

- Prospecting

- Reviewing proposals

- Preparing for presentations

A famous story of a man, Ivy Lee, a management consultant who met with Charles Schwab, the CEO of Bethlehem Steel more than fifty years ago, highlights the positive impact of prioritizing tasks. The consultant offered the following advice: He told Mr. Schwab that at the start of each day, he should list the most important tasks that he should accomplish that day and put them in order of priority. When he completed the first task, then, and only then, start working on to the next item.

The CEO asked how much Mr. Lee wanted to be paid. The consultant said to pay him what it was worth. A couple months later, the consultant received a check for $25,000, which in today's dollars is about $250,000.

Most people work on the "little things" and they don't get to their A-priorities. Preferably, only complete B and C tasks to fill in between making progress on A-priority items.

A B priority example would be taking a contract or marketing materials to a customer or prospect rather than the preferable method of completing this task by mail, courier or delegating it to an assistant. The exception would be to discuss a contract in order to close a sale at that time.

Simply put, what are the critical tasks that must be completed so you can achieve your desired success? This is how you "work smarter, not harder."

TO DO LIST

Priority	Task	Completed

Personal To Do	Calls to Make

ASSESS VALUE OF TIME

Determine the tasks that yield the greatest return on your time. By knowing the value of your time, you can best determine how it is spent.

Using 2000 hours in a year (fifty weeks and forty hours a week), you can easily determine the value of each hour. If you wish to make $100,000 a year, your time is worth $50 per hour.

Work only on activities that yield $50 per hour. If you are filing, typing or performing other tasks that can be completed by someone making $15 per hour, or $30,000 per year, then you are not being effective. Use your time wisely and identify those activities that give you the highest yield.

When considering what should be done, ask yourself, "Is this the best use of my time right now that will lead me to achieving my goals?" If not, do tasks that will lead you toward meeting your objectives.

ASSIGN PROSPECTS A PRIORITY

Just as you prioritize tasks, so should you prioritize prospects, customers and distributors. Assign them A, B or C status so you can better determine how to allocate your time.

The criteria for determining priorities could be a specific amount of new revenue for that account, opportunities for add-on growth or for introducing more products in the future. If the opportunity doesn't meet the criteria, consider turning the prospect over to someone else.

PARETO PRINCIPLE

The 80/20 Pareto Principle simply states that you will derive eighty percent of your results from twenty percent of your activity. That is, eighty percent of your sales will come from twenty percent of your prospects, customers or distributors.

Therefore, you must first identify those high priority prospects and spend eighty percent of your time on the top twenty percent of your prospects.

Also, assess your current customers and distributors to determine those that yield the greatest revenue.

Although some sales people believe sales is simply a numbers game, the high achievers know better. They know that they must focus on the prospects with the greatest potential for now and the future. They also know that they must prepare more diligently for the high priority prospect and customer to ensure that they best represent their solutions.

"What counts is not the number of hours you put in, but how much you put in the hours." Theodore Roosevelt.

Experience has shown that sales reps who make the fewest calls and the most calls are less successful than those who make a moderate number of calls.

The latter are better organized, they qualify their prospects more clearly and better prepare for their presentations. They don't simply want to call a lot of people; they want to talk to the best people.

WORK LOG

A simple but effective method to assess where you are spending your time is to keep an accurate log of *everything* you do, ideally for a two week period, but at least three to four "normal" days.

After doing this, you will typically find that you are spending an enormous percentage of your time on C-priorities.

Date	Time	Activity	Priority

ADVANCE SCHEDULING

Scheduling your time weeks in advance rather than just the next week will pay off handsomely. When you become accustomed to scheduling at least two to four weeks in advance, it allows you the flexibility to meet with prospects and to plan your time better. Poor performing reps wait until Monday to start working on the coming week. That is not for you.

FLEXIBLE SCHEDULING

To avoid conflicts in scheduling and to build in flexible time, the secret is not to schedule more than sixty percent of your time, thus allowing for unscheduled emergencies. Otherwise, you will plan to fail by leaving too little time for unplanned interruptions.

SCHEDULE OFFICE TIME

Just as you schedule time away from the office, schedule your time while in the office for completing tasks such as reviewing large proposals or preparing for sales presentations. If your schedule is too tight, you won't have time to plan, to be effective and to meet your obligations.

TELEPHONE SECRETS

Telephone calls can be the biggest time waster if not handled effectively. Returning calls as quickly as possible illustrates your responsiveness and is expected in today's work environment. However, in order to reduce telephone interruptions, the following methods will improve your efficiency.

Although voice mail is the most likely way to take calls, the best method for handling telephone calls is to take them when received. Caller ID can help screen your calls so you can take them from the more important customers. This shows responsiveness and that you are accessible, and it avoids playing telephone tag yet allows you to focus on other activities without interruption.

Placing and returning phone calls in bunches, rather than one at a time, is an effective time saver, and will avoid interruptions while working on other projects.

"We cannot do everything at once, but we can do something at once."—Calvin Coolidge.

Good times for returning calls are early in the morning, after you checked your messages. Right before lunch is another good time to return calls, as people are in a hurry to eat and are less likely to chat. Likewise, you can't afford to spend too much time talking, as you will likely have a prospect or customer luncheon appointment.

Another good time to return calls is just before leaving for the day to ensure that you are responsive to your callers, and it gives you peace of mind in the evening.

Some people spend time talking about unimportant issues. A good rejoinder when someone asks about the weather is, "Fine, what can I do for you?" If you are placing the call, you can immediately say, "I know you are busy, the purpose of my call is…"

To get off the phone, state that you have another meeting, you are leaving for an appointment or say, "Let me let you go…"

The advent of cell phones can provide more interruptions, but the same techniques apply. Using cell phones without a plan can take up a lot of time and is very costly. Monitor your call activity to ensure that you are spending your time and dollars wisely.

"Never confuse motion with action." Ernest Hemingway.

Many use time going from one appointment to another to respond to calls. This can be an effective time saver but be sure to leave time to think about your next appointment.

The drive time between appointments is a good time to determine what you wish to accomplish, questions to ask, a mental review of your presentation or to give yourself a few moments to think about your activities and family.

DELEGATION

Delegating, whenever possible, is one of the most effective time management secrets. Too often, people prefer to do tasks themselves rather than allow others to complete them. Delegate tasks to others to maximize your effectiveness and develop your staff to assume more responsibility.

Delegate work early in the day so someone else can complete it while you are working on other tasks. For example, they can prepare proposals, collect information, type letters and file materials while you are completing A priority tasks.

Throughout the day, review the work to ensure that progress is being made, make corrections if needed and prepare final materials for distribution.

A sample day may include:
8-9 a.m. Prepare materials for others to complete.
1-2 p.m. Review materials and make changes.
4-5 p.m. Final review and distribute.

Define tasks

Ensure that specific guidelines are provided as to the scope of the job, what should be completed, deadline, format and the expected result. The experience of the staff member will determine how detailed you must be to get the project completed correctly.

Allow each person to uncover new ways to complete tasks. This provides them greater satisfaction and often will result in a better outcome. A good rule is to tell an experienced person what you want, but not how to do it.

Even though it takes longer the first time to delegate work rather than doing it yourself, the quality of the work will improve each time. This will free more time for you to work on higher priority items.

PRIME TIME

Prime time, usually nine a.m. to four p.m., is the best time for selling, meeting with prospects and making presentations.

However, senior executives and other leaders are often in early in the morning and late in the evening and may answer their phone before and after their support staff arrives or leaves. Also, late in the afternoon is a good time to approach them as they are planning their next day.

Non-prime time, such as early in the morning or later in the day, should be used to work on projects, such as reviewing proposals, developing special presentations and following up with others on needed information. List your tasks and prioritize them so you can determine the best time of day to complete them.

The secret is to schedule your tasks in your daily calendar.

PAPERWORK

There are a number of techniques for effectively handling paperwork. Try using the STAR method.

- **Suspense**
- **Trash**
- **Action**
- **Reading**

S-Suspense. Create a file for items that are being worked on, but you don't have all the information yet to complete the task. This could include incomplete proposals for which all the information has not been provided, or a list of things to do, such as solving a customer service issue or reading a proposal.

The secret is to make sure you review the suspense file daily to ensure that all outstanding work is completed.

T-Trash. Throw away any unneeded papers. Don't procrastinate by putting papers in a pile somewhere and think you will come back to them later.

A-Action. This file may include letters, contracts or expense reports for your signature. Your assistant knows it will get your first attention, so it includes only those tasks that need action. For routine paperwork, rather than type a separate reply, simply add a handwritten note on the paper and direct it to others, or return it to the sender.

R-Reading. Designate a file for your reading material so you can easily retrieve it when you have time. Schedule time at the end of each day or two hours each Friday afternoon to review the reading file.

Save articles by tearing them from magazines and putting them in the reading file. When traveling, take the reading file with you. The extensive amount of time spent in an airport is an excellent opportunity to catch up on your reading.

When there is limited time to read all the information, at least skim it to capture the highlights. If you haven't read the materials after a month, toss the material or file it for reference.

Use a check mark

Use the check mark method, whereby each time you touch the same piece of paper, you put a check mark on it. When you get tired of seeing check marks, you will be motivated to do something with it.

Touch paper once

The best method is to simply handle the paper once and move it forward.

FILING SYSTEMS

When you set up a proper filing system, you can move that paperwork from the in-basket to the out-basket and beyond so you can easily retrieve it when needed.

Put an "F" for file on each piece of paper and have it filed so it is out of your way, or take ten minutes at the end of each day to file it. Either have the files in your office or let your assistant handle it. You never know when you might need the information. However, it is important to note that more than eighty percent of paper filed is never needed.

Effective methods for filing and retrieving information include:

Alphabetical order

Set up a separate file for each client, prospect or distributor, or by topic in alphabetical order so the information is readily available.

By subject matter

This might include files such as: federal regulations, state regulations, PowerPoint presentation, sales brochures, contracts, etc.

January-December and 1-31

Handle daily tasks by using the 1-31 daily file system that can be used solely or in conjunction with the January-December system. Put notes, papers, or three-by-five cards as reminders in the file for the day needed and retrieve the file daily to remind you of tasks to be completed.

INTERRUPTIONS

Interruptions can be the biggest time wasters. People stopping by to talk are often the culprits, so it is important to control them.

One method to avoid interruptions is to close your door. If working in a cubicle, put up a sign that politely but firmly states, "Please do not interrupt. Working on high priorities."

With rare exceptions, don't allow interruptions, as it distracts your focus and it takes too long to get back on the same train of thought. You will be making presentations most of your time during the day, so you must schedule time to review and prepare.

You can still maintain a healthy relationship with your co-workers, yet stay focused on your critical tasks. Consider yourself an independent contractor who can make as much as you want, depending on how you use your time.

The word gets around pretty quickly if you are a dedicated sales person. Others will respect your time.

Remain standing

When people come to your office, remain standing and talk with them through their first issue and then escort them to the door when finished. You can suggest meeting for lunch or later to discuss the issue in more detail when you have time. If you ask them to sit, it is tough to get rid of them.

Visit other people

If you need information from someone else, go to his or her office or workstation so you can leave when you choose.

TERRITORY MANAGEMENT

When covering a territory that includes prospects, distributors or clients, inform them of your schedule so they know when you will be in their territory.

Deciding in advance the territory you will be in each week will alert your distributors and clients to know when to expect you.

Moreover, you can plan your travel better to get the best airfares and rental cars and to make more efficient use of time.

PLAN THE NEXT DAY

The last thing to do before leaving each day is to take ten to thirty minutes and review your next day's schedule. This reminds you where you need to be and gets your mind ready for the following day. It can also be used to review your proposals and presentations to ensure that you are fully prepared. It's a great motivator.

PLAN THE NEXT WEEK

For many, scheduling Friday afternoon off from sales is an effective time to review your prospect list, check next week's schedule, complete expense reports, review sales forecasting, for submitting paperwork and to read.

Also, this is an excellent time to review proposals, presentations and other materials for the following week that will provide you peace of mind over the weekend.

Those who follow this plan find that they accomplish more each week and ensures that you are prepared and excited about the coming week.

BALANCE WORK, FAMILY PRIORITIES

Choosing to Cheat by Andy Stanley is an excellent book that describes the value of balancing work and family obligations. It sets the framework for choosing how much time you should spend on work rather than being with your family.

One way to evaluate the time you spend on activities is to ask yourself whether you are spending your time wisely. Are you being productive completing your work or are you talking to others about unimportant issues? The critical question to ask is, is this the best use of my time right now? Sometimes it is that simple.

IN SUMMARY

When you read the books that say you can save two hours a day, you won't believe them at first. But as you apply these methods, you will find that it is true.

You will not only save time, but you will be more responsive to your customers while production increases and you have more time for your family.

TIME MANAGEMENT SECRETS

1. Be more effective vs. efficient.

2. Develop a master list of things to do.

3. Use a system to get organized.

4. Prioritize work.

5. Assess value of time.

6. Assign prospects and customers a priority.

7. Practice the Pareto principle.

8. Complete a work log.

9. Schedule only sixty percent of your time.

10. Schedule office time.

11. Learn telephone secrets.

12. Leverage delegation.

13. Use prime time wisely.

14. Use STAR program to handle paper.

15. Develop an effective filing system.

16. Prevent interruptions.

17. Plan next day/week/month.

18. Balance work and family life.

4

Sales Secrets

○ ○

"One of the best ways to persuade others is with your ears—by listening to them."

—*Dean Rusk.*

KEYS TO IMPROVING SALES

Three key strategies will enable you to improve sales significantly and will result in your company increasing revenue growth at lower costs.

- Increase new sales.
- Sell multiple products during each sale.
- Sell more products to current customers.

INCREASE NEW SALES

Selling a greater number of new accounts is the best way to increase revenue and market share. A sales leader uses targeted sales campaigns, develops strong prospecting skills and creates new marketing opportunities.

The high achiever is often referred to as the "hunter" or "rainmaker," and achieves this status by creating unprecedented sales where others have performed only modestly well. A high performer assesses the potential that can be realized in their market and then develops strategies for achieving results.

Ideal Customer

One of the first steps in maximizing your sales is to determine your ideal customer. That is, which prospects, current customers or distributors have purchased in the past or are most likely to purchase your products? Which ones provide a high average revenue per sale, solid profitability for the company, have a need for additional products and services you offer and have the ability to pay for your service?

Developing your "ideal customer" profile is one of the most critical steps in developing your prospecting plan. If you don't know what you want, you will never know if you find it.

After identifying ideal customers, develop a sales plan to gain access to them.

Identify key prospects

By identifying your best prospects, you can achieve greater success in a shorter time period. This is accomplished by targeting specific prospects, e.g., employers with more than 5,000 employees, more than $100 million in revenue, or small employers with fewer than fifty employees, etc.

List prospects

List your top hundred prospects so you have a manageable number to target. These may vary by city, size or ease of potential sale, but you need a defined list so you can focus your efforts.

Using the Pareto 80/20 Principle, work on the top twenty of your top one hundred prospects, or the key prospects. Focus your energy on your key prospect list and maintaining a top one hundred prospect list.

Research prospects

Once you list your top hundred prospects, begin preliminary research by reviewing the prospect's web site, obtaining names of the top officers and determining whom to approach. You may find that some prospects no longer qualify, so you add more prospects and begin your research on them.

- List top one hundred prospects.
- Research to prioritize prospects.
- Develop sales campaigns.

If you target smaller employers, your approach may be broader, and buying mailing lists or e-mail addresses of specific individuals within a company can be an effective use of your resources. This strategy may result in numerous sales that may be handled best by providing a customer service number to call or a web site where customers may purchase goods directly.

Develop sales strategies

Sales campaigns provide a more programmatic approach to your market and include a systematic follow-up plan. Sales strategies consist of phone calls, letters, e-mail campaigns or advertising directed at prospects. Your campaign may be the same for each prospect or may be completely different, depending on the results of your research.

Sales Strategies

- Set due date and completion dates.
- Identify top one hundred prospects.
- Qualify prospects-A, B or C.
- Contact by mail and phone or visit.
- Visit top twenty prospects within sixty days.
- Identify & contact top twenty customers.

SELL MORE PRODUCTS AT EACH SALE

The second most important strategy for increasing sales is to sell multiple products at each sale. This technique of selling additional products after the buyer purchases one product is typically called up-selling. By up-selling services you dramatically increase the average revenue per sale, and your commissions will increase as well. Up-selling at least one more service per sale can result in an average of twenty-five to fifty percent more revenue per sale.

Typically, products are designed to work more efficiently and at a lower cost when sold together, and offering discounts when products or services are purchased at the same time can increase sales and still protect your margins.

The challenge is to provide alternatives and to make purchasing more products at one time compelling to the buyer.

By researching your prospects and using your discovery techniques you will uncover needs from your prospects that identify opportunities for selling multiple products.

Increasing your productivity, not production alone, is part of your quantum leap strategy, and selling more products on each sale is an effective way to accomplish your goals.

An example is responding to a television ad by calling and being offered the original product but also another two to five more items. Some add-ons could be adding a dryer along with a washer, warranty protection, free shipping with full payment, and much more.

MARKET TO EXISTING CUSTOMERS

Typically, the fastest and lowest-cost method to increase sales immediately is to evaluate your current customer list and determine which would benefit from adding other products and services.

It is six times less expensive to sell to an existing customer than it is to bring in a new one. Selling to a client is cheaper in terms of cost, time and effort.

Your suite of products is usually designed to save the customer money when combined so the customer receives greater value by purchasing additional products.

Customers know you and your company, and if they are happy with the service, they will meet with you more readily and welcome hearing about how other products can add value.

Establishing stronger relationships with your clients will enable you to understand their needs as they undergo changes.

Knowing their corporate strategies will enable you to review your existing customer list to determine where your products or services can benefit current clients.

Review client list

Prepare a printout of the customers in your territory, listing the services they currently have, and determine which other products would provide the greatest value for each customer.

Review existing client lists and identify the top twenty opportunities by ranking your customers, using the A, B, C criteria used for prospects.

Once you know how many customers you have in each of your markets and with each product, you can develop a plan to increase sales into your customer base.

Key strategies for selling to current customers

- Obtain list of customers.
- Review customer list.
- Identify top twenty customers each month.
- Develop sales campaigns.

Schedule time to prospect to clients

Decide whom you will call on first and the secret is to schedule time for prospecting to your clients. Develop sales campaigns to approach them through direct mail, telephone, e-mail campaigns or a combination of these techniques.

Develop a letter outlining other products or services that complement current offerings and the benefit they will provide your client. Where appropriate, arrange for a presentation and prepare for it as if your customer is a new client. Never take a client for granted. Remember, the number one reason clients' leave is that they do not think the vendor appreciates their business.

Build several relationships within clients

You should build relationships high, wide and deep among your clients and recognize that your current contact may be promoted or leave. Often, new people at the client company don't have the same allegiance to you as your prior relationship.

Calling on someone you know results in a faster, less expensive and more positive atmosphere for selling additional products. You also get to know their organization more thoroughly and can understand how your services can help them meet their corporate objectives.

Provide the best deal you can and reward clients for their long relationship. Competitors are knocking on their door; waiting for your service to decline or trying to take advantage of an existing client with higher prices.

Address client issues

Be particularly alert when a concern arises about your product or service and respond quickly and thoroughly to build a stronger relationship.

Or, call your key contacts to review their satisfaction with your current product and determine their future needs. A satisfied customer is more willing to listen to how your other products can meet their needs.

Review client list monthly

Review your customer list every thirty days, and you will find a number of selling opportunities among your current customers. The adjoining chart shows a method for listing customers and assessing their potential for adding business.

In summary

These three strategies of selling more new business, selling more products at the point of sale and selling more to existing customers are the foundation for achieving greater sales results. They will enable you to jump-start sales and provide continued sales success, and should be embraced by all sales people.

Customer Listing

	Customer	Product(s)	Priority
1			
2			
3			
4			
5			
6			
7			
8			
9			
10			
11			
12			
13			
14			
15			
16			
17			
18			
19			
20			

DON'T GIVE UP

Achieving the quantum leap in success requires persistence in following through on sales. Sales people must overcome several objections from their prospect, and the salesperson who continually pursues the buyer typically wins the sale. Marketing studies show that a small percent of sales professionals are persistent in the prospecting process.

45% give up after the first sales call.
23% more give up after the second sales call.
13% give up after the third No.
9% give up after the fourth rejection.

10% continue to pursue beyond four calls.
60% of buyers say No four times before saying Yes.

Conclusion: the top ten to twenty percent of sales people sell eighty percent of all sales.

FOLLOW UP

After sending or presenting your proposal, it is clear that you must follow up with the prospect to determine their level of interest. Set an appropriate time to follow, e.g., twenty four to seventy two hours. Ask if the prospect received the proposal, uncover questions on terms, and identify any issues that need attention.

Determine how your proposal compares to others if there is competition. Seek the "last look," the ability to review the final proposals so you can revise or amend yours to secure the sale.

CUSTOMER SERVICE

Some sales professionals are also charged with servicing what they sell. In the eyes of the customer, they represent the company, and if there are any issues, they look to the person who sold them the product or service to resolve them.

Building a positive relationship by resolving any outstanding issues will reward you with up-selling opportunities, while generating references and referrals for use with new prospects.

In some businesses, sales reps are responsible to resell the service each year, and often this requires presenting a price increase. Others demand continued enhancements or regular service calls to ensure that the client remains happy and doesn't consider a competitor's offering.

- Make regular service calls.

- Make a courtesy visit.

- Respond quickly.

Contact regularly

Some simple methods to ensure that your customers are happy are to call them or visit them on a regular basis, whether quarterly, monthly or weekly.

Enhance your customer relationships by calling periodically to see how they are doing. Take them to lunch to assess progress, send newsletters, holiday greeting cards, birthday cards and emails to stay updated on their company needs.

Be sure to ask your customer service units to alert you if a customer has contacted them with a concern, especially if it has not been resolved. When calling clients allow ample time so if they have issues, you can take steps to resolve them.

Contact customers in accordance with their expectations. Some may not want to hear from you and they want to call you only if something is not working well or they have problems. The easiest and most effective way to determine their needs is to ask them how often they would like to hear from you.

Courtesy visits

Clients appreciate the courtesy of a visit even where there is a dedicated customer service team. Maintaining current customers is far less costly for the company and is a key component of showing continued revenue growth. This step will not only help your company retain much needed revenue but also it will reduce the pressure to sell as much.

Studies reveal that two-thirds of companies that stop using a service do so because of a perception that the vendor does not value the customer relationship. A satisfied customer will remain with your company even through tough times if you pay attention to them.

Many salespeople don't think that it is their job to service the client, and the customer service department should do it. But if one of your sales strategies is to sell additional products to your existing clients, you must make the commitment to professionalism and ensure that each customer is a satisfied one.

When the time comes for adding products, your knowledge and relationship with customers will position you to offer more services, and they will be more willing to buy from a trusted adviser.

Respond quickly

Be sure to respond quickly to customer calls, preferably answering them the same day. Even if you cannot get an answer right away, at least contact them and leave a message that you are working on the issue and you will call them at a stipulated time.

Ask them when they need a response. Some may need it within two hours, as their boss is breathing down their necks, and others may not need a response for a week. Don't assume their deadline.

When you receive requests via letter, telephone or e-mail, it is best to respond in the same manner as the request. If you receive a letter, respond by letter. If by telephone, follow up with an e-mail or letter to document the problem, but if it is a legal question, it must always be documented.

Handling complaints

Too often, sales reps send an e-mail to the home office, saying the Sally Jones at ABC company is having problems getting a shipment, or their claims paid, or a correct billing, and don't add enough detail to identify the action required.

The professional sales person gathers the facts, prepares a comprehensive memo and requests resolution by presenting acceptable options. For example:

Sally Jones at ABC Company, client number 1234567, states that their February monthly bill shows a double entry for item 3654. They received only one order but were charged for two. She is requesting we either credit her account for the extra charge, or send another of the same item 3654 at no cost. She needs an answer by next Tuesday, as she has to close her books for the month. Please send her a response with a copy to me. Thank you for a timely response.

Plan customer service calls

A simple customer service chart allows you to plan and implement service calls quickly. This can be completed at the beginning of each year and updated with new customers.

Simply list all of your customers and then put the months of the year across the top of the chart, and then enter a check mark in the months that you plan to call that customer. When completed, you simply enter the date or fill in the box. See Customer Service chart.

By separating your customers by territory, you can manage your visits better. Some customers who must be resold each year may require you to visit them at least three months prior to the anniversary date.

Moreover, you can achieve more than twenty-five percent of your sales each year through selling additional products to existing customers. And remember, you will retain more clients just by showing them that you care about them by contacting them regularly.

Your sales force automation system can be invaluable in preparing your customer list and scheduling your calls.

When you schedule time for planning, be sure to consider calls on customers equally as important as calls to prospects and distributors.

There are "acres of diamonds" among your customers, and they are worthy of your time and attention. They can pay huge dividends and reward you highly for providing them what they expected when they bought your products. Good customer service.

As Brian Tracy says, "there is no traffic jam on the extra mile."

Customer Service Planning Chart

Client	J	F	M	A	M	J	J	A	S	O	N	D
1												
2												
3												
4												
5												
6												
7												
8												
9												
10												
11												
12												
13												
14												
15												
16												
17												
18												
19												
20												

SALES SECRETS

1. **Increase new sales.**

   a. **Identify ideal customer.**

   b. **Identify key prospects.**

   c. **List prospects.**

   d. **Research prospects.**

   e. **Develop sales strategies.**

2. **Sell multiple products per sale.**

3. **Sell to customer base.**

   a. **Review client list.**

   b. **Schedule time to prospect.**

   c. **Build several relationships within client.**

   d. **Address client issues.**

   e. **Review client list continually.**

4. **Don't give up.**

5. **Follow-up.**

6. **Customer Service.**

   a. **Contact regularly.**

   b. **Respond quickly.**

   c. **Handle complaints.**

   d. **Plan customer service calls.**

5

Marketing Secrets

You will achieve greater sales by developing a marketing plan for approaching your target market among your customers, prospects and distributors. Some of these methods include mail campaigns, telephone techniques and direct calling.

MARKETING STRATEGIES

Defining your marketing strategies as to who, what, when, why, where and how you will approach each prospect will help you identify sure-fire methods to target your market successfully.

To ensure that you accomplish your sales goals, develop marketing campaigns to support each sales initiative. If you have a marketing department, it can assist in the process. Marketing campaigns may include using advertising, mail campaigns, telephone programs, trade shows and working through your distribution channels.

ADVERTISING

Use the yellow pages, business journals, newspapers and business cards to advertise your business. Depending on your business, using mailers to neighborhoods offering discounts for first visits can develop long-time paying customers.

"Doing business without advertising is like winking at a girl in the dark. You know what you are doing, but nobody else does."—Stuart H. Britt.

Track your sales results directly to your advertising campaigns by assessing which ads work best, where your best customers are located and what they purchased. Coding ads and then asking for the code when a purchase is made can trace the origin of the promotion.

By profiling the success of different ads, you can determine where and how to spend advertising dollars and can plan future sales campaigns that yield greater results.

DIRECT MAIL CAMPAIGNS

A well-designed direct mail campaign targeted at several people within a prospect can reap great rewards. In his excellent book *The Power to Get In*, Michael Boylan describes a number of methods and advantages to a focused letter campaign.

Michael Boylan was a musician that was extremely successful in gaining access to senior executives. They were not as impressed with his music as they were with his ability to secure appointments with the highest officers of the music business. They, in turn, recommended he describe his unique talent and he did in his insightful book.

High and wide approach

Start at the highest level in the company and work down whenever possible. High and wide best describes the approach for targeting key executives. You want to reach as high in the organization as possible and target many top executives, often four or more to ensure that everyone who may be affected by your service is aware of its benefits.

In spite of e-mail and other new prospecting methods, sales letters remain an important part of effective sales campaigns. Maintain the focus on the benefits the prospect will receive by reading your letter and responding to it.

Headline benefits

Grab their attention with a headline or opening sentence describing what a prospect or customer will gain by reading the letter. Can you save them money, reduce their staff, improve quality, lower their costs, and increase the speed to process and so forth? The reader will be interested if you can provide specific benefits that will help their business.

Become an expert letter writer

Review books on effective letter writing or hire an expert to position your product so it compels the reader to want more. The best-selling book, *Selling to VITO* by Robert Parinello, contains excellent ideas on how to approach top executives among your prospects.

Letters can help qualify prospects by providing an overview of your product set and offer an incentive for them to call you, to go to your web site or take your follow-up phone call.

Another method is to send a letter to your customers providing a specific solution and determine if they have any interest in discussing it. When you call them later, they will know the intent of the call and are prepared to discuss the service.

TELEPHONE SKILLS

Telephone campaigns are an integral part of a successful sales person's prospecting program both in conjunction with prospecting letters or as a stand-alone initiative. An effective telephone skill is often the most important trait that separates successful sales people and the also-rans.

Call reluctance can be overcome with a well-designed and rehearsed telephone presentation. Some key components of an effective sales call are:

- Provide your name.
- Name your company.
- Ask for time to speak.
- Provide a power statement.
- Ask if you are talking to the appropriate person.

The first thirty seconds in a phone presentation, like a headline in a letter, must highlight key points that you want the listener to hear: the headline, the grabber, and three key benefits that would warrant them talking with you.

The secret is to make a perfectly rehearsed message so each word motivates the prospect to talk with you. Know the purpose of the call, know what you are going to say, prepare answers to common questions and ask for an appointment or the order.

- Have a solid opening.
- Develop a headline grabber.
- Uncover needs.
- Provide benefits to address need.
- Develop responses to common questions.
- Include a call to action.

Phone power training courses are available and can be found in sales magazines. Telemasters is an outstanding program with years of experience and success.

Write presentation
Writing out your telephone presentation and practicing it aloud will help you improve the content. If you simply call and make something up, it will be clear that you have not prepared, and future calls will be ignored.

Develop opening

Your opening will often determine your success. You must get to the point and provide a benefit to the listener. Some comments to avoid are the chatty, "Hi, how are you today?" Followed with "That's great."

Rather, start with "I am James Smith with ABC Company, and we have an offer that will enable you to reduce your costs and increase your sales. Am I speaking to the appropriate person who has responsibility for these benefits?"

Qualify prospects

The successful rep qualifies prospects in order to secure an appointment with a person who needs your product, who can afford it and who has the authority to buy. With a few quick but vital questions you can save endless hours traveling and making a presentation only to find there is no need.

Create next steps

A call to action requires the caller to insist on developing a next step. Whether it is to send a proposal, set an appointment or make a follow-up call, an action should occur to move the sales process forward.

VOICE MAIL CAMPAIGNS

Since most people receive more than ninety percent of their phone calls on voice mail, your presentation must generate enthusiasm and interest in your product or service. Although you will have a direct conversation with only about ten percent of those you call, be prepared when someone answers the call. Your presentation should be planned, rehearsed and presented in a convincing manner.

Broadcast messages

Also, an effective way to reach more prospects is to use a voice mail messenger system that can widely broadcast your prerecorded message.

Using this service allows you to leave a thirty-to forty-second voice mail message on various subjects.

You simply prepare your message, provide phone numbers for prospects and record your message for distribution.

Vendors such as Boomerang, Boxpilot and others can leave hundreds of voice mail messages with the last one sounding as fresh as the first.

Increase appointments

The telephone can increase your appointment ratio and qualify prospects more effectively. The professional knows that time is money, and using the telephone will increase appointments to qualified prospects and is the essence of his or her success.

Webinars

Webinars are becoming more popular, allowing sales people to make their presentation to prospects located throughout their territory. Typically, an announcement of a webinar can be sent to prospects or clients informing them of the subject matter and how it can benefit them and their company. The cost is relatively low, travel costs are avoided and listeners can remain in their offices.

It is best to present information on innovative product enhancements, regulatory changes or other issues that are not viewed as simply pushing a product.

TELEMARKETING FIRMS

Telemarketing companies can be extremely effective in using proven techniques to set appointments, sell products and to increase the time in front of qualified prospects. They also can test-market your product prior to hiring a large sales force.

TRADE SHOWS AND SEMINARS

Attending trade shows and speaking at seminars can generate a number of leads to be followed on and qualified. Providing a drawing for a gift can generate a number of business cards in a bowl for follow-up.

Be sure to assess the value of the show and determine what you are attempting to accomplish, e.g., showing your support for an industry organization, reaching current customers, building brand awareness or developing new prospects.

Understanding your goals will help determine whether to sponsor the event, what materials to bring and your level of participation.

CUSTOMER REFERRALS

Seasoned sales veterans obtain referrals from satisfied customers in order to reduce the need for cold calling. The confirmation of having performed successfully with a number of satisfied customers and distributors goes a long way in leveraging these relationships into new customers.

Obtaining referrals, or leads from existing customers who identify others who may be able to use your service, is an inexpensive method to obtain additional business. Your satisfied clients may provide referrals to other companies or individuals whom they know in the industry or community.

Referrals are worth their weight in gold. You can use referrals to gain access into other businesses that means fewer or no cold calls in your future. In turn, you will spend more quality time in front of qualified prospects that will lead to more sales.

The secret to obtaining referrals is asking for them as they are usually not offered freely, but when asked, clients are often willing to provide them.

TESTIMONIALS

Letters, quotes or survey results from customers provide testimonials that can be used with new prospects to show them that you provide excellent products and services. Put these in protected plastic covers so they last a long time and are fresh when making presentations.

Obtaining testimonials becomes easier and more helpful in the sales process when your company has high customer satisfaction ratings. Your good service work and caring for the customer will result in obtaining testimonial letters that can be shown to other prospects.

Customers will often provide testimonial letters that praise your products and services but are uncertain how to prepare them. You can simplify the process of obtaining testimonial letters from customers by providing a draft of a referral letter and suggest they add or delete whatever they think is appropriate. This technique simply gives them a head start, yet they feel the letter is their creation.

Testimonials can be gathered from your clients, distributors or your company's customer service unit, and often replace the need for prospects to contact references.

REFERENCES

A happy customer is more likely to provide a letter of reference recommending you and your company that is invaluable in building credibility with other prospects and overcoming objections.

In most large Requests For Proposals (RFPs), references are required and it is vital that you have several quality references to use when needed. Having a number of references by size, by industry, by service, etc. allows you to tailor your references based on the type of business you are pursuing.

Also, by having a large number of references, allows you to use different ones as a client is typically happy to provide occasional references, but it can be annoying when called on frequently.

MARKETING PLAN

A marketing plan should be developed annually and reviewed quarterly to ensure that you remain on track. Including all these items in your plan will remind you to use these time proven secrets that have enabled other sales professionals to achieve greater success.

Marketing Strategies:

- Letter campaigns
- Phone calls
- Webinars/seminars
- Telemarketers
- Referrals
- Testimonials
- References

Determine which strategies will be used, develop specific plans for completing each strategy and include defined dates for completion.

"Happiness consists in activity—it is a running stream, not a stagnant pool." John M. Good.

The secret is to develop these action plans continually and updating them as your specific market needs change. Be consistent in your approach and you will find all these strategies can be used effectively throughout the year.

MARKETING SECRETS

1. **Develop marketing strategies.**

2. **Advertise.**

3. **Use direct mail campaigns.**

    a. **High and wide.**

    b. **Headline benefits.**

    c. **Become an expert letter writer.**

4. **Develop telephone skills.**

    a. **Write presentation.**

    b. **Develop opening.**

    c. **Qualify prospects.**

    d. **Create next steps.**

5. **Voice mail campaigns.**

    a. **Broadcast messages.**

    b. **Increase appointments.**

    c. **Use Webinars.**

6. **Consider telemarketing firms.**

7. **Attend trade shows.**

8. **Conduct seminars.**

9. **Obtain referrals, testimonials and references.**

6

Prospecting Secrets

If you ask top sales persons what makes them successful year after year, they will tell you that prospecting is the number one activity they plan to do each week.

PLAN TO PROSPECT

Scheduling time for prospecting is the first thing a successful rep should plan each week, and nothing should get in its way.

Of course, if a sale is pending and it interrupts the scheduled prospecting, then you should complete the sale but reschedule prospecting for another time that week.

Prospecting for leads can be the most difficult or the easiest part of your selling process. Typically, when starting your sales career, you work harder to obtain leads. As you become more established, your lead source will grow and referrals from customers will expand.

Increasing your sales "funnel" or "pipeline" on a continual basis will provide a steady stream of sales opportunities.

Mediocre sales people will generate a lot of activity and work those leads until they make some sales. After they make a couple of sales, they have to start their funnel from scratch and lose valuable time, production and income. Conversely, the sales professional will prospect continually, producing a list of qualified leads to follow.

Prospecting methods that can support your marketing campaigns include:

1. Identify and research target market prospects.

2. List all prospects in a database.

3. Qualify prospects by A, B and C.

4. Contact each within sixty days.

5. Visit the top ten prospects in each city by end of next quarter.

MARKET ANALYSIS

The first step in building a full funnel is to identify your key prospects. There are a number of lists that can be purchased that identify prospects by industry, profession or by zip code.

These lists include the employers' or individuals' names, addresses, SIC codes, number of employees, and sales/revenue so you can compare them to your ideal customer profile.

Define target market

An important aspect of prospecting is defining your target market. Whether it is all steel manufacturers or software suppliers, determine who they are, and which ones have the greatest potential.

Another purpose of defining your market is to enable you to better manage your territory. For example, rather than spend the same amount of time in each city, pinpoint where the greatest number of opportunities are and spend more time and resources in those select markets.

If you sell to distributors, who resell your products, know their market potential and how they can market your products more effectively. Evaluating your entire territory can determine where your best prospects are located.

Part of your market analysis is to ask yourself some basic questions:

1. Do you know your market share?
2. Have you broken down your market by size?
3. Where are your best prospects located?
4. How many people live in each market?
5. How many companies in each segment?

For example, you may want to prospect to all companies in a certain industry within sixty miles of Chicago that have sales of more than ten million dollars and employ more than five hundred employees.

Identify markets

Perhaps your best target market is a balance of small, medium and large prospects, or maybe you should only focus on a select market. Your market may dictate selling to a lot of small companies or just a few large ones, or to individuals.

Your success will improve as you identify and qualify prospects in order to target your ideal prospect. It is vitally important for you to know to whom you are going to sell. Once you determine your ideal markets, sales strategies can be developed to engage them more readily.

Market Analysis

Name:
Date:
Target Market:
    Industry
    Annual revenue
    Other

Market Segments: Size of prospect   Location
Demographics
    Population
    MSA (metropolitan statistical area)
    State
    Counties
Market Share:
    #Prospects
    #Clients
    # Using each service
    %Share

Prospect Information:
    List prospects
    Key contacts
Competitor Information:
<u>Name</u>   <u>USA</u>   <u>Strengths</u>   <u>Weaknesses</u>

MARKET SEGMENTS

Determine market segments by size of prospect in terms of number of employees, annual sales or need for products. Focus your energy on those key prospects, and identify where your top hundred prospects, customers and distributors are located.

Target Companies

City	Population	1-100	100-1,000	1000+

BUSINESS SOURCES

Gathering background information from a number of business sources will ensure that you are effectively screening out low return suspects and focusing on high return prospects.

Some of these sources include:

- Public library
- Chamber of Commerce
- Department of Labor
- Dun & Bradstreet listings
- Judy Diamond for insurance
- Business USA business lists
- The Book of Lists published by the top forty city Business Chronicles or Journals

PROSPECT RESEARCH

The old method of securing an appointment and then asking the prospect about his or her company is no longer effective. You are expected to gather information on the prospect and understand the company background and nature of their business.

Hoovers, Lexis-Nexis and Dun & Bradstreet are valuable sources of specific company information that provides background so you understand that prospect's services, locations, financial data and more. This step is necessary for you to make a preliminary analysis and effective overture.

You build credibility with a potential customer by knowing their quarterly results, being aware of their recent merger or that they are introducing a new product.

By completing research beforehand, you are prepared to ask more relevant questions, put issues in their proper context and not waste an executive's valuable time.

CUSTOMER REVIEW

Vendor management is becoming a challenge to companies, as they have to work with a number of providers for similar or related services. If you can reduce that number by providing a total solution, you will gain more business. And you can typically offer favorable pricing when customers buy more than one of your products.

There are options on how to approach prospects. One option is to ask prospects, customers and distributors for thirty minutes of their time to review your entire product line so they know what can help them achieve their goals. This option positions you in a consultant role, providing the client more alternatives to consider at that time or in the future.

Another option is to approach them with a single solution integrated with an existing one. This second option shows the customers that you have reviewed their needs and can pinpoint a solution that offers value to them.

If your presentation is proper, and your products are superior, clients will welcome the greater efficiency while reducing the number of vendors they have to deal with.

PRE-CALL PLAN

Develop a game plan prior to making sales calls. Be specific. Know the objective of each call. In short, it is to move the prospect down the sales funnel from suspect, to prospect, to ideal customer status.

Plan for each call by determining what you need to know about the prospect. If it is a first call, your research will provide you the background information that will lead you to questions that will allow you to prepare a detailed proposal. Some examples:

- Can you be specific on your revenue goals?
- Are you introducing new products?
- How do you view staff training?
- Do you plan a major investment in systems?

Know the intent of each call and always be prepared to provide a substantive idea that will further peak their interest.

DISCOVERY QUESTIONNAIRE

Identify the prospect's needs by developing and completing a comprehensive discovery questionnaire. In turn, your proposal can provide solutions to help prospects achieve their goals.

Understand the prospect's needs by knowing the company's challenges and how your solutions can help solve them. Are they facing a layoff, have they selected a new computer system, do they have new management or expect to undergo a reorganization?

During the discovery process, determine the person who has the authority to buy. Also, identify those who can say no to your proposal. For example, the CFO may have the final say, but the systems people can kill the deal.

In John MacKay's book *Swim With The Sharks*, the sixty-six questions his salespeople use help to gather needed information to build relationships with prospects and customers.

Your discovery document should not only include the company challenges and identify specific needs, but also the name, address and phone number of key people, but also, very importantly, birthdays, names of their children, anniversaries, hobbies and more.

Discovery Questionnaire

Name:

Address:

Phone: Cell: Email: Fax:

SIC: Industry:

Employees:

Annual Sales:

Current Vendors:

Business Challenges:

What they like in vendors:

Systems Challenges:

Budget Allocated:

Decision Makers:

Sense of Urgency:

Solutions:

Hobbies:

Spouse:

Children:

DEVELOP SOLUTIONS

Depending on what you determine from discovery will help shape your recommended solutions. The solutions may not only result in your products being purchased, but also may require partnering with another company to help solve a unique problem, perhaps even before they purchase your products.

Remember that people don't buy products and services. They buy solutions to their problems.

Maybe they need a solution for all their branches around the country rather than just the local one. This extra step may result in a much bigger sale, as you can provide them a quantity discount and switch the entire company to one solution. This is also why you have to read and stay up to date on industry changes.

MANAGE DISTRIBUTION CHANNELS

Brokers and manufacturers' reps can be effective distribution channels to remarket your products and services. They typically are paid a fee or commission, but it lowers your direct cost of acquiring new business and gets into more accounts faster.

Determine which distributors you want to do business with by doing some research. Don't wait for a distributor to send business your way.

Know who all the key distributors are and develop a strategy to meet them. There are likely many that you have not met who can provide you a lot of referral business.

Develop a list of all the distributors in each city in your territory by reviewing your current customer list and identifying the distributor who brought your company the business. Also, use industry journals and local resources to locate the key producers.

Plan your work and work your plan.

Identify top producers

Control your destiny by seeking out those who control a lot of the business in your markets. Treat distributors just like prospects and sell them as you would any other prospect. That is a different approach from the way most sales people do their job, but it will set you apart.

By aligning your products and services with those of your distributors, you are better positioned to reap greater rewards. Ask probing questions as to the products the distributor represents, identify their primary vendor, determine the level of training among their sales force, and ascertain what it would take for your products to be their leading ones.

Apply the eighty-twenty Pareto principle and recognize that twenty percent of your distributors will provide eighty percent of your leads and sales. Don't treat all distributors the same. Spend eighty percent of your time marketing to the top twenty percent.

Like advertising, tracking results by each distributor will ensure that you maximize your effort on those that yield the greatest return on your investment. Prioritizing them will enable you to identify quickly those who will provide the highest number of leads.

- What is their target market?
- Do they work with certain industries?
- What size companies do they work with?
- What do they want from a service provider?
- Do they base their recommendations on price, commissions, and references, or other factors?
- Do they tend to favor one vendor all the time?

COMPETITION

Knowing your competitors' strengths and weaknesses as well as their pricing and product strategies is invaluable and enables you to highlight your advantages while minimizing their strongest points.

Identify competitor's strengths and weaknesses

Identify your top five competitors? List their five major strengths and weaknesses, pricing strategies, and their unique selling advantage (USA). In short, why do they get business when you don't?

Some competitors use price, innovative products, customer service or other features as their selling advantage.

An excellent book, *The Discipline of Market Leaders*, by Michael Treacy and Fred Wiersema, declares that companies tend to be best at one major benefit, but often not more than one. They can be the most innovative, or have the best service, or lowest prices, but rarely all of those.

Don't ever knock your competition. Point out the strengths of your product versus your competitors. When you speak poorly of your competition, you weaken your position in the eyes of the prospect. In some instances, you may convince the prospect not to buy anyone's product.

Know competitor's niche

Just as companies such as Nike, IBM or Wal-Mart have their special niche, so should your company, and you must know how to exploit your market advantages.

Your marketing department may be able to provide detail on your competitors, but it is important for you to gather competitive information and summarize it.

Determine the strengths, weaknesses and USA of your major competitors.

COMPETITOR ANALYSIS

	Competitor	USA	Strengths	Weaknesses
A				
B				
C				
D				
E				
F				
G				
H				
I				

DEVELOP PROFESSIONAL RELATIONSHIPS

A favorable relationship with a prospect is often the critical difference when selecting a vendor. As more products become commodities, your relationships make a big difference in your sales results.

Methods to build better relationships include inviting prospects to sporting events, monthly newsletters, sending birthday and holiday cards and, most importantly, contacting and visiting them regularly.

One of the most important ways is to become their "trusted adviser," that is, one they can count on to provide them current information and advice on what is best for them, regardless whether it is your product or not.

In some instances, your professional relationship will extend to a personal one as well. This is ideal but will not always happen. Learn to distinguish them and be mindful that most senior executives maintain an arms length between professional and personal relationships.

JUST SAY NO

Inform your prospect when you cannot meet their expectations if your company does not provide the requested service. Some companies don't fit your criteria and never will. Be considered a trusted consultant to that prospect and they may buy from you anyway, since other competitors may also not be able to meet their expectations.

Let your distributors know what you can provide and save time from reviewing unwarranted proposals. If you continually turn down a number of prospects that distributors send you, your distribution channel doesn't understand your market niche.

Define product scope

Make it crystal clear what your company is really good at, and you will increase your close ratio and help your distributors as well.

Assess what percent of your current business you turn down because you can't meet the prospects' criteria or they don't meet the specifications of your products. Perhaps the prospect is too small, their credit rating is poor, or they want custom products and yours are standard.

Yes, you may send prospects to your competitors, because it is the right thing to do for the customer, and your prospect or distributor will appreciate your honesty.

Be prepared to walk away

Sometimes the best sale you make for the company is the one you walk away from. You avoid causing internal operational difficulties by selling the "one-off" solution that your company cannot service, that is a money loser and, ultimately, the customer will be unhappy and leave.

Occasionally, you will be challenged when prospects don't meet the "ideal customer" criteria, and you will have to decide whether it is worth the investment of time to pursue that opportunity.

Know what your company can and cannot do and represent that in your marketplace and you will be successful. The products you sell will meet the needs of many, but not all prospects; so don't fall into the "first year mistake" category by selling something you cannot service.

Once your distributors or customers know your sweet spot, they will want to do business with you because they can count on good service and the product meeting their needs. This is a win-win for everyone.

PROSPECTING SECRETS

1. **Plan to prospect.**

2. **Prepare market analysis.**

3. **Establish market segments.**

4. **Use business sources.**

5. **Complete prospect research.**

6. **Review customer list.**

7. **Have a pre-call plan.**

8. **Develop discovery questionnaire.**

9. **Prepare business solutions.**

10. **Manage distribution channels.**

11. **Identify competition.**

12. **Develop professional and personal relationships.**

13. **Say No to bad business.**

7

Presentation Secrets

"Winston Churchill has spent a lifetime coming up with a spontaneous remark."

—Unknown.

The ability to make effective presentations is an art form everyone can master with a little practice and some helpful tips and can elevate your sales success as well as your career.

One of the major factors, and often the leading reason, for continued success is the ability to present products to solve a problem. You become more confident, more credible and your audience will appreciate your professionalism.

Grabbing their attention, creating interest, generating desire and motivating the prospect to action sum up the purpose of your presentation. Use the **A-I-D-A approach.**

A-Attention
I-Interest
D-Desire
A-Action

The number-one challenge facing today's decision makers is having the time to complete their work. When you are prepared to make effective and concise presentations, you will be rewarded with the prospect awarding you the business.

"Let your discourse with men of business be short and comprehensive." George Washington.

Making successful presentations is not all about standing in front of a lot of people and making a speech, although that can be part of it, and it can be an enjoyable part once you are comfortable with your topic.

Rather, you will be called upon to make presentations in a number of different settings. Most successful presentations vary from one-on-one to a small group, to a committee or to a board of directors. The techniques used can vary, but the themes of preparation, practice and rehearsing are common to all.

It seems that all sales reps, regardless of experience, fall into a comfort zone when making presentations. You could make them in your sleep, right? The problem is that your prospects pick up on that and they become as unenthusiastic as you are.

Let's review the basics of what it takes to make eye-popping presentations that lead the prospects to buy, to utter those famous words, "Where do I sign?"

PLANNING PRESENTATIONS

The next important phase of making effective presentations is the planning stage. Assuming you know who will be in the meeting and what key buying points to make (saving money, reducing staff, meeting quality standards, improving service or tackling pricing issues) let's review how you make a presentation that sets you apart from your competition.

This is the planning step, where you determine what you are going to say, how to present it and what salient points you will make to compel the prospect to consider your services.

Abe Lincoln said that if you wanted a good twenty-minute speech, he needed two weeks to prepare. If you wanted a forty-minute speech, he needed only one week. But if he could talk as long as he wanted, he was ready at any time.

Regrettably, many sales reps think they are going to "fake it until they make it," and they fail in their presentations. Rather than take the time to prepare, they would rather blame the lost sale on price, product features or customer service. Often they were outsold because they didn't adequately prepare for that presentation or make a convincing enough impact on the buyer.

KNOW YOUR INTRODUCTION AND CLOSE

It is imperative that your opening and your close are rehearsed to the point that they are memorized. Don't take a chance or "wing it," as it will show the prospect you have not prepared for them, and you may say something that does not quite fit and ruin your entire presentation.

Just like the airline pilot whose biggest challenge is the take-off and landing, so is the opening and closing of your presentation.

In order to grab the audience's attention and keep it, you must adhere to a few rules. One, make your introduction less than two minutes and make it so compelling that if they heard nothing else, they would want to buy your product. Present benefits only in your opening comments.

For more than forty years, the Dale Carnegie course has been teaching people how to be more effective by giving speeches in less than two minutes. It is surprising how much you can say in that short period of time when you are prepared.

KNOW YOUR PRODUCTS

One of the major problems challenging sales people is knowing and understanding their products so they can recite the features and benefits readily, and position products so they are aligned with the client needs.

When students take a college course, they often memorize the content, but if asked to apply that knowledge, they cannot. It is absolutely critical to know your products inside out and be able to present them professionally and without hesitation.

Some newer reps make joint sales calls with their sales managers, and as they listen, they think they can handle the presentation. But when in front of a prospect, the words don't come as easily as expected.

Compare this approach to singing along with a song on the radio. As long as the music is playing, you can sing along with the words. But, if you turn down the volume, can you continue to finish the song? When it comes to your products, you should be able to pick up on any feature or benefit and finish the presentation.

Only when you can finish the presentation on your own, just like finishing the song, will you truly be in command of your sales presentations. This takes practice, and it becomes even easier if you are the writer of the song or, in this case, your own sales presentation.

> *"If I miss one day's practice, I notice it.*
> *If I miss two days, the critics notice it.*
> *It I miss three days, the audience notices it."*
>
> —Andrew Paderewski; Polish pianist-statesman.

PRESENTATION TECHNIQUES

Knowing the fundamentals of making a good presentation will give you greater confidence and enable you to make a more favorable impression.

Overcome Fear

Although public speaking is the greatest fear of most people, there are many options available to improve your skills. Toastmasters, Dale Carnegie and other local public speaking seminars are resources that should be employed to ensure you possess the most professional approach.

Smile

One of the first and most important things to do when making any presentation is to smile warmly. It sets a positive tone. Remember that people do business with people they like. Be friendly.

Power Position

When making presentations, position yourself so they all face you, so you can see their reaction when you are making your points. Take the appropriate place at the head of the table or in front of the room.

Check set up

Arrive early to ensure that the presentation room is set up with the appropriate equipment such as an easel, flip chart and power for your computer.

Check everything out in advance; even a walk-through of your entire presentation would be appropriate. You may find that you picked up the wrong presentation, that the changes you made for company A did not get replaced and would not show well for company B. Ensure that the equipment is compatible and it can run with your computer.

Stand to Make Presentations

Stand up to present your product whenever possible. Studies show that those who stand and use visual aids have a higher close ratio and sell at a higher price than those who sit and present.

In David People's book, *Presentations Plus*, he cites a study done at the University of Minnesota that showed when presenters stand and use visual aids, they are forty-three percent more effective in persuading the audience. Moreover, people are willing to pay twenty-six percent more money for the same product or service.

When standing, learn to stand still, without pacing or leaning on a chair or putting your hands in your pockets and juggling your change. These are distracting and divert the listener's attention away from your message.

- Use visual aids.
- Stand up to present.
- Keep hands at sides.

Your feet should be about shoulder width apart, your weight evenly distributed on both feet and your hands at your sides except when making a point.

Notice that people doing commercials on television keep their hands at their sides so they don't distract the viewer. It takes discipline, but it is worth it.

When you are nervous, speak slowly and clearly. This will give you the breathing control needed for a professional presentation.

REHEARSE PRESENTATIONS

Many sales reps, when asked to practice their presentation, protest that they don't want to memorize it. The answer is not to memorize your presentation, but to *know* your presentation.

When you know your presentation thoroughly, you will experience greater success and never be intimidated by any audience.

If you are interrupted with questions, you should be able to handle them effectively and get back into your presentation without missing a beat.

An effective test to determine how comfortable you are in presenting your products is to allow other sales reps to call out any one of your products and you make a presentation and handle their questions?

One technique to challenge you is the two-hat method. That is, if your sales manager put all your products and a list of all sales reps and pulled a product and your name at random, would you be prepared to make a presentation to other sales reps, respond to questions and close the audience. If you are not prepared, then you have some work to do.

The most important thing you can do to prepare is to practice. You must rehearse your comments and have them prepared to the slightest detail, such as your stories or examples.

Practice at home in front of a mirror or with your spouse as your audience. Videotape yourself to see how well you present. Practice with your peers—your toughest audience—and allow them to ask the tough questions. You will notice a significant improvement in a short time.

POWERPOINT PRESENTATIONS

Some use PowerPoint presentations that show the prospect background facts about your company, features and benefits and key selling points about your products and why they should buy from you.

The disadvantage is that reps tend to make the same presentation to everyone, neglecting to customize for each prospect to make it meaningful and memorable. Moreover, the PowerPoint presentation is used as a substitute for a compelling message. Too often, this canned presentation is too long, and puts your audience to sleep. It can lull them into a state of anxiety, wondering how long they must endure the presentation.

If your audience is large or you are appealing to many buyers and need to show your technology, PowerPoints can be extremely effective for delivering your message. Be sure it is tailored to meet the prospects needs, not yours.

Limit text

Secrets for making your PowerPoint presentations more effective include using only five bullets per page and only five to seven words per bullet. Otherwise, each page is simply too busy and many will lose interest.

Often, less professional presenters simply type sentences on their slides and read them verbatim. Rather, they should use bullets, and illustrate each point with an example, story or anecdote.

Computer screen facing you

Another annoying habit to avoid is to turn your back to the audience to read the bullets projected on the screen. To avoid this, have your computer screen facing you so you can refer to it readily during the presentation.

When presenting your PowerPoint, use an LCD (Liquid Crystal Display) so everyone can view the information easily.

Some companies that you present to have LCDs available in their work place, so it is not always necessary to purchase one and lug it around. Simply ask in advance if they can make one available for your use. If you need to purchase one, the newer models are much lighter, but still expensive.

Effective Presentations

- Use PowerPoint.
- Limit-five bullets per page.
- Limit five to seven words per bullet.
- Don't read bullets verbatim.
- Position laptop to read screen.

EASELS

Easels can be highly effective for using bullets; listing key points and diagramming to illustrate your ideas more effectively. Always have one available, so you can respond to questions and write out key words and phrases. It is a lifesaver if your electronic equipment fails.

When using an easel as part of your presentation, prepare your key points in advance and put them on subsequent pages and flip to them when needed. The audience does not want to watch you write out your presentation.

David Peoples provides this tip: If you must add key points during your presentation, one method is to write out the ideas in pencil in advance. As you present, simply write over them so you don't have to refer to your notes. This appears more spontaneous.

PERSONAL INTRODUCTION

One technique that will set you apart from others, that loosens up the audience and allows you to make a better connection, is to provide a more personal introduction.

Rather than use the same impersonal approach of giving your name, title and job responsibility, try adding more background information on yourself.

For example:

"Hello, I am John Smith in charge of sales. I grew up in Naperville, Illinois, and graduated from Northwestern with a degree in business.

My wife Sandra and I have two teenage children. I have been with ABC Company for seven years, responsible for sales and marketing, and my hobbies include golf, hiking and tennis."

Establish the goals of the presentation and request for input as to what the audience would like to gain from the presentation.

Personal Introduction

Your Name_____
Title/Job_____
Home Town_____
College_____
Hobbies_____
Family_____
Goals for today_____

If each participant takes thirty seconds to provide a like introduction, you will find more common connections with your prospect in the first twenty minutes than you would over the next year. Try it.

UNIQUE SELLING ADVANTAGE (USA)

Begin the presentation by framing your USA, your unique selling advantage. Some call this your unique selling proposition or power positions, among other names.

If the prospect remembers only one thing, it should be what sets you apart from your competition. Some USAs may include: nationwide distribution, money back guarantee, best warranty, lowest cost, highest quality, etc.

A different approach to defining your products and services is described in the book, *Purple Cow*, by Seth Godin. That is, how can your product stand out from others and be totally unique in the marketplace? Seth Godin is a best-selling author, public speaker and has started several successful companies. This is a book to read for everyone, not just sales people.

Include the key benefits as a constant reminder.

UNIQUE SELLING ADVANTAGE (USA)

USA:_____

1. Benefit_____

    a. _____

    b. _____

    c. _____

2. Benefit_____

    a. _____

    b. _____

    c. _____

3. Benefit_____

    a. _____

    b. _____

    c. _____

PRIORITIZE BENEFITS

Present the three strongest benefits your product offers that meet the prospect's highest needs. The most important benefit should be first so if you get interrupted your prospects will know your major benefit.

The third most important point should be second, and the second most important point should be third. Bookend your key benefits. People remember the first thing and the last thing you say.

Develop three major selling benefits. Add three more bullets to support each of those key points, resulting in nine more good reasons for the prospect to buy. For example, under saving money, you could add low price, reduced staffing costs and a money-back guarantee.

When you spend a few minutes on this approach, you can come up with even more sub-bullets under each sub-point to provide more benefits of your product or service.

To distinguish between features and benefits, simply think about the difference between what your product does and what it can do to alleviate your prospect's pain.

For example, your washing machine may have a number of amps (feature) that will save you time to wash your clothes and reduce the cost to operate the machine (benefit).

The tires on your car may have deeper tread (feature) to last longer (feature) so the cost is less over time (benefit).

If someone mentions a feature, ask, so what? You should get a benefit for an answer.

PROOF STATEMENTS

Be prepared to prove any of the statements you make, so prepare them in advance. Cite specific articles or studies from which you obtained your facts, and don't ever make something up. If you don't know or cannot provide factual information, simply make a note of it and tell them you will get back to them later, or don't present it until you have done your homework.

STORYTELLING

As important as it is to know your products and be able to present them in a logical order, you must also make them come alive by telling stories, sharing experiences or giving examples of how your products actually benefit other customers. Read a testimonial letter from one of your satisfied customers on how you saved them money, reduced their time or responded to their needs with timely customer service.

OVERCOME OBJECTIONS

Once you prepared, rehearsed and made your presentation, you will enter into the sales portion of the presentation, the handling of objections.

Prior to making a presentation, write down the five most common objections you receive. Now, write down an effective response that places your product or service in a positive light. Each time you make a presentation, write down new objections and responses to remain current.

Review them later and determine if you can improve them and build them into your Q & A library. Soon you will have the top twenty or more frequently asked questions (FAQs) and excellent responses.

- List five common objections.
- Develop written responses.
- Add more objections and responses.

When responding to a question, pause, restate the question to ensure that others heard it, and then respond. This brief pause will give you time to collect your thoughts and frame the response in a positive manner.

Even though you may have heard the same question a hundred times, respond by saying, "That is a very good question," and provide your answer. It makes the person asking the question feel respected and also provides time to prepare your response.

Sometimes, prospects will ask questions to which they know the answers, but want to test you. Don't fall for it by making something up, or you will lose any opportunity for this or any subsequent sale.

As your products and services change, update your FAQs in more detail. With a little time and practice, you will gain the confidence to win more sales by being able to overcome objections. See adjoining chart.

When making your presentation, it is usually best not to provide handouts prior to the presentation, as your audience will page through it while you are talking and won't listen as intently.

In some instances, especially when more technical information is provided or you want the audience to take notes, it is appropriate to provide them materials in advance.

FAQ'S (FREQUENTLY ASKED QUESTIONS)

- Question_____?
- Response_____
  _____

- Question_____?
- Response_____
  _____

- Question_____?
- Response_____
  _____

- Question_____?
- Response_____
  _____

- Question_____?
- Response_____
  _____

SUMMARIZE

When finishing your formal presentation, summarize the key points that you want the audience to remember.

Remember to highlight your USA and key benefits that will enable the prospect to satisfy their objectives.

THE CLOSE

The final step in the presentation is to develop the close. Developing your close before you begin will help position the sales presentation toward your end goal. To gauge how the audience responded to your presentation is to simply ask them, "What do you think, or what are your thoughts?"

This open-ended question will allow the prospect to respond and provides you information on how to proceed, which leads to your next questions; "Where do we go from here, or what are the next steps?"

Closing questions will enable you to develop a sales strategy for your next meeting or will enable you to close the deal at that time or soon after.

When the solutions match the prospect's needs, the close moves to asking about the effective date, delivery date, when to begin implementation, and so on. A simple question such as "When do we start?" may be all that is needed to move the process forward.

Yes, you still use closings such as the "puppy dog," in which you invite the person to try something at home for a few days or weeks. The Ben Franklin method of listing the pros and cons is still valuable. These techniques are typically built into your proposal and presentation rather than used during the typical close.

FOLLOW-UP ON LOST SALES

One method to determine why you lost a sale is simply to call the prospect and ask why they bought from somebody else. In some instances, it may be that you could have made a better presentation, but it is hard to get that from prospects, as they don't want to embarrass you.

"Diligence is the mother of good luck." Benjamin Franklin.

One secret is to ask them how you could have improved your presentation, and they will often tell you.

Then it will be up to you to develop your skills or let your sales manager know the training you need to improve your capabilities.

As Andrew Carnegie said, *"The first man gets the oyster, the second man gets the shell."*

The most successful sales people are those fully prepared when making presentations. It can move you from being one of the finalists to the company of choice. By adhering to these principles, you will become successful in sales presentations that will yield more sales and a greater income.

PRESENTATION SECRETS

1. Plan your presentation.

2. Develop personal introduction.

3. Know introduction and close thoroughly.

4. Know product features and benefits.

5. Use proven presentation techniques.

6. Rehearse presentations.

7. Use PowerPoint.

8. Easels provide flexibility.

9. Develop USA.

10. Prioritize key benefits.

11. Provide proof statements and stories.

12. Overcome objections with FAQ's.

13. Summarize.

14. Close.

15. Follow up on lost sales.

8

Negotiating Secrets

o o o o o o o o o o o o o o o o o o o o o o o o o o o o o o

"Let us never negotiate out of fear but let us never fear to negotiate."

—*John F. Kennedy.*

The ability to negotiate a successful contract is a very important aspect of successfully closing profitable business for you and your company.

Average sales people lead with their best price; assuming that the incumbent may already have a low price and they don't want to lose the sale from the onset. You want to make it to the second round.

Other times, prices may be spread-sheeted and you don't have much control over the bidding process. Spread sheeting is when your services and prices are listed and compared to your competitors without much personal involvement from the sales person.

Haggling over terms and price is expected. Position yourself with your customers and prospects to ensure that you can negotiate the terms of your contract. The following provides some methods for coming out on top, while the customer still benefits from your services.

Negotiating is often perceived as one person or company winning while the other loses. Often this is true but it is because those involved are not skilled at negotiating tactics that enables each party to be successful. Here is an example of how a customer can pay more for something and feel better than a person who paid less.

Let's assume you are selling a product for $2,000 and your prospect says, "I'll offer you $1,500 for that item." You respond, "Okay, I'll take it." What happened? The person who bought the item felt he or she could have gotten it for less money by offering even less, and may even question the quality of the product. You are concerned that you acted too quickly and afraid that your boss is going to accuse you of being an order taker and not a true salesperson.

Now, on your next sale, after you have learned all about your product, you approach the sale much differently. The next prospect says to you, "I'll offer you $1,500 for that $2,000 item." You respond, "Oh no, I couldn't let you have this item with its beautiful craftsmanship and quality for less than $1,900. It has a lifetime guarantee and we provide free installation." The prospect counters at $1,800, and you agree on the price of $1,850. Now you and your boss are happy and the customer thinks he made a good deal. That is an effective negotiation.

WHY PROSPECTS BUY

Always put yourself in the customers' shoes to determine what they want out of the deal. After your initial discussion with your prospect, you should have a good idea as to why a person or company would want to buy your product or service.

Before you go into negotiations, list at least the five reasons why you think the prospect would want to buy your product. You must be prepared to negotiate on each point, whether it is price, service, warranties, time of delivery, systems support or a host of other issues.

WHY PROSPECTS BUY

Reasons Why People Buy My Service.

1.

2.

3.

4.

5.

6.

7.

8.

9.

10.

11.

12.

13

14.

15.

16.

KNOW VALUE OF PRODUCTS

By learning all the features and benefits of your products and the value of each, you are better prepared to negotiate each feature. In some instances, specific features may not be provided at any cost as the special handling creates higher costs than the value of the service, and the resulting service provided would be less than acceptable to the customer.

Although most sales people still feel that price is the most important reason people buy, it isn't. Studies continue to show that price is usually ranked about fifth as to why people buy.

- Reputation of vendor.
- Quality of product.
- Salesperson's relationship.
- Customer service.
- Price.
- Financial stability of vendor.
- Breadth of services.

PREPARE NEGOTIATING POSITIONS

In reality, you must be in the ballpark with your pricing to begin the buying decision. When you know that price will be an important consideration, it is important to know:

1. The highest price that you would like to sell your product for at which you achieve full margins.
2. The price you are willing to accept.
3. The walk-away price.

Most companies establish pricing models that include full margins, costs to add additional features and ad hoc pricing for special requests.

The successful sales person fully understands their companies pricing model and will be able to value each service.

Most importantly, know when you are prepared to walk away, that is, when it doesn't make any sense to complete the deal under their terms.

Remember, not all people in business play fair, and sometimes the best deal is the one you walk away from.

Just as some opportunities sound too good to be true, some deals have you asking, why are we doing this? If the deal doesn't feel right, step back, consult with others and then revisit the issue on new terms.

ESTABLISH PRICING STRATEGIES

If people always bought products for the lowest price, everyone would buy the cheapest car, cheapest house or cheapest washing machine. What they want is the best value for their money. By knowing the value of your products you can justify your price compared to the competition.

Compare the features being offered under your prices and those of the competitors. Your pricing may include a three-year warranty, but your competitor's warranty may be priced separately. Some prospects may require special systems work, so define what is included in your price.

Sometimes you have to assess whether the prospect will buy at your price or whether you agree to lower your price to compete with lower-priced brands. Does your company want to be the lowest priced product and not have all the features of the high-end competitor? Or is your target market at the high end of quality, features and price?

Your company may be willing to give up some sales, assuming you have presented your value proposition and defined your target market.

Other times, you might match the lower price to gain market share. If you stick to your high-end pricing, you may eventually get that business if they competition doesn't deliver on their promises. In short, know your company's pricing strategy and its target market.

Remember that if you win business on price you will lose business on price.

Some competitors use predatory pricing to enter a market, to build market share, or in desperation, to add revenue.

But after the sale they don't provide the level of service your company does and they may increase prices in subsequent years. It is important to know your competitors' pricing strategies and determine an effective strategy to compete with them.

"The bitterness of poor quality remains long after the thrill of a cheap price is forgotten." Unknown

Identify ten or fifteen features, such as systems interfaces, delivery dates, the cost to revise the product and so on. All features need to be assessed from the ideal sale to the walk-away point, and each of these features may be used in place of price to negotiate your best deal.

LINE-ITEM NEGOTIATION

Whenever possible, avoid negotiating by line item. That is, don't agree to a lot of little things in the order presented. Discover what the other person wants in total. If you have given most of your chips away early and then they come in for the close, you will have nothing left to negotiate.

You always want to keep a few small features that you can give away later to sweeten the deal. This is best accomplished by saying "I understand your position on that, but let's come back to it later," and keep all those features as part of your list so you can determine their priority.

Be prepared to give away less-costly items for little or no money, but reserve the more expensive items to trade on price or to satisfy the key need of the prospect.

Those who ask for more, get more.

Another secret is to reduce the price on the one product if they purchase the second one at the same time.

NEGOTIATE IN SMALL INCREMENTS

The secret is to give up only one percent at a time, not ten percent. Too many sales people are prepared to give away too much right off the top, thinking that the buyer will jump at the chance to close the deal. In fact, the buyer thinks that if it was that easy to get a discount, she is wondering how much more you are willing to give up.

For each percentage that you give up, ask to reduce the number of features provided. For example, "We can lower that price, but which of these features would you like to eliminate?"

OMIT WEAK ARGUMENTS

When negotiating an issue, never present a weak argument as part of your negotiation. If you have three strong points, then present only those three points. If you present a fourth point just to throw it in, your opponents will attack that issue and you will spend most of the time on that issue and lose credibility on the other three.

HIGHER AUTHORITY

Effective negotiating tactics include using the 'higher authority' or 'time out' strategies. When heavily engaged in negotiations, and a number of issues are being discussed, and it becomes confusing, step back to assess all the issues by stating that you don't have the authority and must consult with others.

This may or may not be true, but this strategy will give you and your team time to regroup and reconsider all the issues in a less pressured environment. Using a time out provides leverage in closing by letting the buyers know how much authority you have. If they want to close the deal that day they must be willing to accept less favorable terms. For example, if the buyers want immediate delivery they may be more likely to accept your terms.

This tactic works for a buyer as well. You call for a time out and meet with your staff separately to assess the situation. You can step out of the room and pretend to call your boss to get authority that you already possess. This can help speed up the buying and selling process.

WIN-WIN

The most successful negotiations result when you achieve a win-win outcome, where you have a satisfied customer and your company prospers. By negotiating successfully, you not only satisfy the goals of your company, but you also solidify professional relationships.

The ability to negotiate successfully through the sales process positions you for greater success. Good clients understand and appreciate that you are giving them favorable terms while still supporting your company values. And finally, you will build stronger customer relations that create opportunities for more business in the future.

NEGOTIATING SECRETS

1. **Identify why prospects buy.**

2. **Know the value of products.**

3. **Prepare negotiating positions.**

4. **Establish pricing strategies.**
   a. **Provide value, not cheapest price.**
   b. **Know your company's pricing strategy.**
   c. **Know competitors' pricing strategies.**

5. **Don't line item negotiate.**

6. **Negotiate in small increments: 1% vs. 10%.**

7. **Omit weak arguments.**

8. **Use higher authority or time outs.**

9. **Strive for win-win.**

9

Communication Secrets

o o o o o o o o o o o o o o o o o o o o o o o o o o o o o o o

"People Don't Care How Much You Know
Until They Know How Much You Care."

—John C. Maxwell

Effective communication can be the most important aspect of your business. You write letters to prospects and customers in order to grab and keep their attention. You talk with prospects and distributors to understand their needs in a short period of time. You communicate within your own company through the home office, your boss and others. How well you use effective communication skills will determine how successful you will be in your career.

Be an effective communicator in writing, personal interaction and listening. Your business requires that you possess each of these traits, and you must do them all very well. Make the commitment to ensure that your correspondence is thorough and professional.

The secret of communicating effectively is to always proofread your correspondence prior to sending. The sooner you resolve this issue in your sales career, the faster you will receive favorable responses and a better outcome for the customer.

This chapter will address how to prepare effective letters and memorandums, proper email usage, and key techniques for developing listening skills.

THANK YOU

After a new sale is complete, the professional sales person sends a thank-you note to those who purchased services. More importantly, a phone call within sixty days of the purchase is a must to ensure that the new client is satisfied with the service purchased.

Remember, a happy customer purchased something; an unhappy customer was sold something.

AVOID MISSPELLING WORDS

Avoid them by using spell check, grammar check, and especially by rereading your correspondence prior to sending. Just as spelling errors are inappropriate for writing letters to prospects and clients, so it is within your own company when using e-mail, memos or reports.

Errors reflect poorly on the sender, showing that the writer has not taken the time to ensure that his or her communication is proper.

Commonly misspelled words

- Lose vs. Loose. You lose something, but something is loose.

- Role vs. Roll. Your role in the company is important. You roll the ball.

- Compliment vs. Complement. You can receive a compliment. Your product can complement the others.

- Their vs. There. Their is person-related. There is a location.

- i.e. means that is.

- e.g. means for example.

LETTER WRITING

Headline grabs attention

State the purpose of a letter early, even to the point of starting the letter with a headline. Just like a good headline in the newspaper can tell you the main point of the article, so does the opening in a letter. Try writing the main point of your letter in eight words or less. For example, "INCREASE SALES BY FIFTY PERCENT AND REDUCE COSTS."

Executives are too busy to plow through paragraphs to get to your main idea. They want to know why they should take the two to five minutes to read your letter. Save for later the history of your company and how many customers you serve. Get to the point.

WIIFM

Your reader is asking "WIIIFM." What is in it for me? If you can address that question in the first paragraph, it is likely that your letter will be read.

Can you express clearly why that prospect should read more than the first paragraph? Will you save them money, reduce their staffing costs, provide them freedom from hassles, or a host of other critical issues?

Include powerful words that attract attention. These have proven to evoke positive responses. Some of these include:

- Guarantee

- Proven

- Reduce

- Save

- Quality

- Advantage

- Value

Provide benefits

In the body of the letter, provide immediate and compelling reasons to create a high level of interest so they will continue reading. One of the best ways is to provide only benefits that the reader will receive. Example: Our ability to reduce the cost of manufacturing can result in lower prices, higher sales and greater profits for your company.

Call to action

Be sure you include a "call to action," that is, a statement at the end of the letter that asks them to take action; to make a call, look up your website, respond by fax or expect a call. This creates an expectation and moves the sales process forward.

Try the simple exercise of reviewing your letters to see if they meet these important criteria. Ask yourself if you were the reader, would you continue to read the letter? If it doesn't grab *you* immediately, rewrite your letter.

Bad news letters

If the letter contains bad news, soften the blow by placing the bad news in the middle of the letter surrounded by other information that assures the reader that you carefully considered the issue, that you ran it by your corporate legal staff, etc.

Stating that you evaluated the issue and cannot provide a full refund, but would be willing to give a discount on their next purchase is preferable to simply saying you can't help.

MEMORANDUMS

Memo writing is an art form that few possess. The secret is to provide your purpose in the first sentence and other points in a logical sequence, with background detail and other information to support your request.

Example: I am requesting a five percent price concession on product H for the ABC Company, as they are current customers for three of our most profitable products and have an excellent payment record.

Keep your memos to one page or less and include only pertinent information. Leave out the unimportant details that simply slow down the reader and the process.

- Include purpose in first paragraph.
- Keep memos to one page.
- Provide details so action can be taken.

A number of people may be involved in reviewing your memos, so provide enough details to support your key points, such as the impact on marketing, pricing, billing, manufacturing and how these areas could be affected.

Unless your direct boss can approve your request, assume that it will travel to a number of people throughout the organization.

COVER MEMOS

Salespeople are constantly reminded to include a cover memo when sending information to the home office, especially when the prospect's needs are different from the standard product offering. Without specific information, the home office cannot properly evaluate or implement the opportunity.

Provide detailed information

If the information is incomplete, the reader will not fully understand what is being asked and your company will not do what the client requested.

When you request an exception or a different design from the standard, those making the decisions will often hedge their quotes and not give you the best price or options unless your request includes detailed information.

Provide as many facts as needed and add your perception of what the prospect truly wants. Include why the prospect is considering a different vendor and what specific issues will motive them to buy.

If the home office works with the customer and discovers that the information provided by you was incomplete or incorrect and customization is an added cost, the relationship with the customer is off to a bad start.

Always answer the following questions to ensure that the content contains enough information for someone to understand your message fully.

Who?   **When?**

What?   **Why?**

Where?   **How?**

Studies continue to show that it takes twelve good deeds to overcome one bad experience, especially when it is a new customer. Help the process by providing complete and accurate information.

One idea per paragraph

Superior memos contain only one idea per paragraph and that each idea flows in a logical sequence. The best method is simply to jot down all the ideas you wish to convey, organize them in order, and then write the memo.

Prepare a summary of the key points, especially what the client was looking for, the critical issues, and the motivation for the prospect to be looking for a new vendor.

Otherwise, others assume the decision is based on price, and that is not always the reason for switching vendors.

Using this secret will help you clearly communicate your message and result in faster and more complete responses.

E-MAIL USAGE

E-mails have become the method to communicate virtually all messages to include the company strategy, human resources policies and everyday communication. However, e-mail is also becoming a stranglehold on the ability to get things done.

Often, very little thought is given to composing e-mails versus memorandums. Too often, emails have typos, poorly worded sentences and readers are asked to review other attached emails to understand the topic.

The following secrets will improve the use of e-mail and greatly enhance their effectiveness and your efficiency.

One issue per e-mail

People often include a number of issues under one e-mail heading. This makes it difficult to retrieve or to respond, as sorting by subject will not identify the issue if it is included with other e-mails.

When the issue is important and you anticipate follow-up, type separate e-mails by subject, and it will save you and others a lot of time in the long run.

Combine e-mails

Rather than forward a string of e-mails on the same subject, combine them so the next reader, who often is your boss, can understand the issue without having to piece together a number of other e-mails. Your action will be appreciated, and you will receive a more timely response.

Assume wide distribution

Assume that your e-mail will be sent to everyone in the company, including your boss and the CEO. Provide the facts, include all sides of the issue, frame the problem, and request a specific solution.

Limit distribution

With the increase in the number of e-mails, send them only to the people who need to read them. It is not necessary to copy the world and have everyone else review them.

Avoid inflammatory comments

Your communication must be free of any inflammatory comments. That is, don't say, "I wish all the people in the home office had a brain so our customers could get something from them." This will turn off anyone from wanting to help, and likely the request will go to the bottom of the pile.

You should write your correspondence so if it was on the front page of the newspaper, you would not be embarrassed.

"Never answer a letter while you are angry."—Chinese proverb.

Simply stating the facts and requesting a resolution will go a long way in getting others to assist in resolving the problem.

All too often, letters, memos or e-mails cannot be passed on to others and have to be rewritten, as they contain inflammatory language. Assume that your e-mail will be sent throughout the organization, so soften it to make your point and be less abrasive and more professional.

When you are upset, use the pause technique before you express your anger. Prepare your thoughts on paper and set it aside for an hour or more and then reread it, eliminating those words or sentences that are inflammatory.

- Provide detail on each e-mail.
- Combine other e-mails.
- Assume e-mails will be distributed widely.
- Avoid inflammatory comments.
- Reread emails prior to sending.

The secret is to reread e-mails to ensure they convey the proper message before sending. Be sure that the editorial comments are eliminated and your intended message is clear. Pretend that you are sending them to one of your best friends and your tone will soften.

EMPLOYEE COMMUNICATIONS

Communication among employees sets the tone of the company. Establish a process that enables each person to communicate his or her ideas, opinions and concerns openly.

Professional communication should occur among all sales, home office and field staff. Whether this is from management to employees or the reverse, proper communication is often the most overlooked but required component of a smooth-running operation. This trait will help ensure that all employees work together toward common goals.

Plan correspondence

People resent others presenting a number of issues in random order without a coherent message. Rather, they appreciate clarity on stating the issue, providing different points of view and a recommendation. The professional prepares ideas thoroughly and presents them in order of priority and states a recommendation or resolution.

Be sure to give careful thought to how your message will be perceived and consider the reader before sending it.

Problem-solving

An effective method to use for resolving issues is the PAR techniques that can provide assistance and for communicating the solution to your prospect, client or distributor.

- P is for stating the Problem, clearly and concisely.

- A is for the Action that has occurred or should occur to solve the problem.

- R is the Result or Resolution you want or have achieved.

SALES MANAGER COMMUNICATION

Sales persons should respond to requests from sales managers quickly. Some of these requests include: completing activity and sales reports, preparing expense vouchers, assessing market trends, updating competitor information and other requested items.

The old expression that the sales manager's priority is the sales rep's priority is still true today as it has been for many years.

Often, your sales manager is requesting information because his boss is requesting it from him. As Zig Ziglar, a prominent sales trainer and author of many books on sales, said, "The way to get what you want is to help others get what they want."

Seek assistance

Don't hesitate to approach your boss if you are struggling. Be proactive in calling your sales manager and inform her that you are not meeting quota. Explain what you are doing to correct the shortfall or ask for advice on how you can improve.

Your sales manager is paying attention as she not only reads the sales reports, but so does her boss. They are giving you time to improve, and your calling to discuss the issue is perceived as a positive sign.

Just like the astute student requests feedback and assistance from their teacher, sales reps should seek out the advice of their sales managers and other leading sales reps to determine how they can improve their sales results.

For example, you may notice that another sales person made a sale similar to the one you are pursuing and you could learn their strategies for closing the deal.

"You can't build a reputation on what you are going to do."—Henry Ford.

Take some time to think through specific action steps that you can take to improve your sales. Review the ideas in this and other books to develop a comprehensive sales plan that will result in improving sales.

Be proactive in communicating with your sales manager so she knows that you are eager to learn and that you want to improve your sales results.

Your sales managers can provide feedback and suggestions on how to improve. Don't wait for your annual review. It is too late.

Review progress

Review reports on key sales activity, identifying significant prospects and providing sales strategies for the coming months. This illustrates that you know what is happening in your territory and that you are actively working your market.

Compare your sales results and activity to that required by the company, and don't do it because you have to. Do it because it will provide feedback on what you are doing and whether you are meeting expectations. This review will show if you have contacted your key prospects, distributors and customers.

Review reports

Take the time to review reports them so you are aware of how you are doing compared to your goals, and look for ideas on what you could improve to enhance your performance. Use reports as learning tools.

Communicate with management

- Complete requests on time.
- Call your manager to discuss issues.
- Seek ways to improve results.

IMPROVE LISTENING SKILLS

The most critical communication happens between you and your company and the person who pays the bills—your customer.

Prospects are a close second, as they are your future customers and your ability to communicate effectively with them develops a rapport that often cements the relationship.

In addition to your letter communication, e-mails have become more common, but the most important method is verbal communication.

An important secret for being effective in the communication process, especially in sales, is to listen.

One of the most disturbing attributes of a sales person is the urge to talk rather than to listen to the prospect.

"You can close more business in two months by becoming interested in other people than you can in two years by trying to get people interested in you."—Dale Carnegie.

Listen intently

As vital as listening is when selling, it is even more important when handling customer service issues. Focus on the customers' needs and truly understand their concerns. Gather as many facts as possible about the complaint, the person involved, the date and time, and what the customer would like done.

When listening, focus your attention on the caller, and don't get distracted with e-mails, reading or reviewing your to-do list.

Sales professionals recommend that the sales person talk about one-third of the time and listen to the prospect two-thirds of the time.

Ask questions

Asking questions is the most effective tool to ensure that you get others to provide you information that will enable you to make better decisions when preparing your proposal, pricing and sales strategies.

Too often, the sales person is not listening to what the prospect says, but thinking about what they are going to say next. Avoid that trap.

The sales person often misses what the prospect is saying and continues to give his or her "standard pitch." In turn, the prospect thinks that the sales person isn't there to listen to their real need, but is there simply to sell his or her products.

Focus, ask questions, and you will gather the information needed to resolve the issues.

The information you gather from the prospect will enable you to understand their needs, resolve their problems and determine how that prospect can benefit from your services.

Take notes

Engage in what the prospect is saying and take good notes. This shows the prospect that you are truly interested and also provides excellent background for preparing your final proposal.

In summary

The information gathered by listening will improve the sales and customer service process and reduce the time to complete the needed paperwork.

IMPLEMENTATION

After selling a new account, ensure that all the required information is included when you forward it to your implementation team so the sale is processed smoothly. When details are missing that are needed, the implementation process will suffer. Of course, the faster it moves in the home office, the faster you get paid.

When closing the deal with a customer, provide them with an implementation plan, particularly if it is a more complex sale. Review the steps that will be taken, when each step will occur and what is required by all parties to ensure a smooth and timely receipt of your product or service.

This extra step will comfort the customer and the staff who participate in the purchase, so they know when they can expect the services that were purchased.

Moreover, this plan will be a guide to your implementation team as to the commitments made to the client.

- Provide needed information to the home office.
- Develop an implementation plan for clients.
- Build a comfort level with the customer.

IN SUMMARY

Effective communication is being respectful of the other person by providing them comprehensive information in a succinct manner to facilitate the sales and service process.

Capture the readers' attention with headlines and benefits that are directed to solving the prospect or customers concerns.

Use the guidelines for preparing memorandums, cover memos and emails by limiting each paragraph to one idea, avoid using inflammatory comments and combining emails to make it easier for the reader to understand your topic.

Improve your listening skills by talking less, asking questions and taking good notes. Improving your listening skills will greatly enhance your chances of success by understanding the prospects' needs better and enabling you to provide a more relevant proposal, presentation and implementation plan.

By using effective communication techniques you will find that your time spent is dramatically reduced, the response from others will improve and your sales will increase.

COMMUNICATION SECRETS

1. **Send thank you letters to new clients.**

2. **Avoid spelling errors.**

3. **Proofread all correspondence prior to sending**

4. **Be effective in letter writing.**

    a. **Write key idea as a headline.**

    b. **What's in it for the reader?**

    c. **Provide benefits.**

5. **Email guidelines.**

    a. **One topic per email.**

    b. **Combine emails.**

    c. **Assume wide distribution.**

    d. **Limit distribution.**

    e. **Avoid inflammatory comments.**

6. **Improve listening skills.**

    a. **Listen intently.**

    b. **Ask questions.**

    c. **Take notes.**

7. **Provide implementation plan to client.**

Summary

By adhering to the principles in *Sales Secrets*, you can become a sales professional who surpasses all expectations. Reviewing this book periodically and completing the charts regularly will provide the guideposts for achieving your goals.

Although *Sales Secrets* provides important information, sales professionals will continue to expand his or her knowledge by reading books, listening to audiotapes and attending seminars and training programs.

Committing to success by writing down goals, mirroring others' techniques and gaining a mentor all help to jump-start you toward meeting your objectives.

Automation can help you become more productive by increasing selling time while improving your planning will dramatically increase sales productivity.

Breaking down goals into smaller amounts show that yearly goals can be achieved by completing specific tasks each day, week, month and quarter.

Tracking specific sales activities reveals progress and compares your results to your ideal work level.

Using proven time-management techniques can provide the needed focus to assure success. Listing projects and prioritizing them helps you complete the most important tasks.

Scheduling time to complete A-priorities, avoiding interruptions, handling paperwork once and using a systematic filing system enables you to be more productive.

Simply selling more accounts cannot ensure success; rather, selling multiple products during each sale and adding services to existing clients are keys to increasing your sales results.

Marketing campaigns consist of targeting key prospects and developing effective letter and phone-call campaigns. Identifying an ideal customer is the first step in preparing effective direct mail and telephone campaigns.

A professional letter begins with a headline that states the purpose of the letter and draws the reader to continue reading. Providing benefits to the reader and a call to action are part of an effective letter.

Just like a letter takes preparation for it to be effective, so does a telephone call. The opening will state the purpose and benefit of the call. The first ten seconds are critical to capturing the listener's attention and knowing what you are going to say throughout the call to lead that person to take action is critical in achieving the desired outcome.

Successful reps prospect each week to produce a steady stream of qualified leads. Qualifying leads ensures that you spend your time on those with the greatest potential.

Sources used to identify prospects include: Chamber of Commerce, Department of Labor, Book of Lists, Dun & Bradstreet, Business USA and others.

Hoovers and Lexis Nexis are excellent sources for gaining background information on clients and prospects.

To solidify your prospecting, be prepared with testimonials from happy customers, and references upon request.

During the discovery process you will identify the key reasons the prospect is considering buying. Position your product so it meets all needs, and know when it no longer makes sense to pursue a prospect.

Prior to making your presentation, identify your major competitors and compare their strengths and weaknesses against yours to overcome objections and position your proposal more favorably.

The keys to making effective presentations are to be friendly and to know your subject matter by carefully planning your presentation, rehearsing it and knowing your open and close.

Although PowerPoint presentations are now overused, they can be effective in large groups as a guide. Maintain interest by using few words and not reading from the screen. Provide a unique personal introduction, stand up to present and use an easel to highlight key points.

Provide proof statements, add stories to support key ideas and be prepared to respond to questions by developing the most prevalent objections and responses.

At the end of your presentation, summarize the key points, ask the prospect for their response to the ideas presented, and move toward getting commitment by asking for next steps.

Effective negotiating skills enable you to advance from being an order-taker to a sales professional. Key techniques in negotiating are: avoid line item negotiating, give very little at each request, and backing away to consult with others to assess your current position.

Communicating effectively is the cornerstone of your success with prospects, distributors and within your company. Letters, e-mails, or memos must be concise, yet provide detail so others can understand the issue fully. Know that your correspondence may reach throughout the organization.

An important aspect of communication is the ability to listen to others, gain a full understanding of their objectives and share with them what you heard to gain agreement on the issues.

Using the techniques in this book will enable you to surpass your prior achievements and provide continued success for your entire career. Please use these ideas and those found in the reference books and tapes to achieve your potential. I am confident you will find great success using these *Sales Secrets*.

Best of success to each of you!

References

BOOKS

Ziglar—On Selling
Zig Ziglar

The One Minute Sales Person
Spencer Johnson, M.D.

The Power To Get In
Michael A. Boylan

The Time Trap
Alec Mackenzie

The Organized Executive
Stephanie Winston

Getting Things Done
David Allen

Presentations Plus
David A. Peoples

Secrets of Power Negotiating for Salespeople
Roger Dawson

Hope Is Not a Strategy, The 6 Keys to Winning the Complex Sale
Rick Page

How To Become a RAINMAKER
Jeffrey Fox

Selling to Vito, the Very Important Top Officer
Anthony Parinello

THINK and SELL like a CEO
Anthony Parinello

Advanced Selling Strategies
Brian Tracy

HOW TO WIN CUSTOMERS AND KEEP THEM FOR LIFE
Michael LeBoeuf, Ph.D.

The Sales Bible
Jeffrey H. Gitomer

How to Master the Art of Selling
Tom Hopkins

Spin Selling
Neil Rackham

Purple Cow
Seth Godin

The 21 Indispensable Qualities of a Leader
John Maxwell

The Seven Habits of Highly Successful People
Stephen Covey

The Power of Focus
Jack Canfield, Mark Victor Hansen, Les Hewitt

AUDIOTAPES

How to Master Your Time
Brian Tracy

Advanced Selling Techniques
Brian Tracy

The New Strategic Selling
Stephen E. Heiman and Diane Sanchez

Low Profile Selling
Tom Hopkins

Swim With The Sharks
Harvey Mackay

TIME MANAGEMENT SYSTEMS

Franklin Covey
Day Timers
Planner Pads

PERSONAL DIGITAL ASSISTANTS (PDA)

Palm Pilot
Blackberry

SALES FORCE AUTOMATION SYSTEMS

Act!
Goldmine
Maximizer
Pivotal

0-595-30192-4